The Sunday Times

Woodland and Wildflower Gardening

THE SUNDAY TIMES

BOOK OF

WOODLAND

AND

WILDFLOWER GARDENING

GRAHAM ROSE

DAVID & CHARLES

Newton Abbot · London · North Pomfret (Vt)

British Library Cataloguing in Publication Data

Rose, Graham
Sunday Times Book of Woodland and Wild flower Gardening
I. Shade-Tolerant Plants — Great Britain
I. Title
635-9'54   SB 434 7

ISBN 0-7153-9112-7

Designed by Grub Street Design, London

Illustrations (except designers' own plans) by
Alison Hainey
Illustration on page 6/7
Shirley Ffelts and The Sunday Times
Photographs by Insight Photographic
except for pages 84, 124 David Quigley; pages 2/3, 69, 80 John Glover; pages 96, 104 Michael Warren

Printed in West Germany
by
Mohn Books GMBH
for David & Charles Publishers plc
Brunel House, Newton Abbot, Devon

Phototypesetting by Chapterhouse Ltd,
Formby, L37 3PX, England
Published in the United States of America
by David & Charles Inc
North Pomfret, Vermont 05053, USA

CONTENTS

FOREWORD 6

Beautifying a small plot of land, much of which is overhung by the canopy of a neighbour's tree, might seem like a daunting task for debutant gardeners. They will soon discover that the major problem to be overcome is establishing plants in shade. The tree roots, too, will add to the difficulties because they will tend to keep the soil beneath the tree exceedingly dry.

Similar handicaps have to be tolerated by

Clematis montana

Geranium
pratense

Hedera helix

Primula vulgaris

Iris laevigata

suburban or rural gardeners with larger plots whose land is surrounded by tall hedges in which mature trees predominate. But, instead of bewailing their misfortune, gardeners in these circumstances should view their situation with equanimity because the offending trees could turn out to be a priceless asset if the garden is designed to take advantage of the natural shade they offer.

All trees which are tall enough to become so dominant are beautiful natural phenomena which can impart great character to a garden and their shade can provide the broken light which some of the choicest of garden plants enjoy. Certainly, anyone who has faced the task of making an attractive garden on a barren site would envy the good fortune of people troubled by the presence of nearby tall trees. Most of them would probably decide to allow the trees to dictate the whole character of the surround to their home by opting to make a romantic woodland garden; and, because such a style of gardening is both low maintenance and among the most charming, even on their own bare plots, many of them would opt to try as quickly as possible to erect the leafy high canopy which trees and tall shrubs provide, by using the expensive techniques of instant gardening and actually planting semi-mature trees.

Just what can be achieved under both sets of circumstances was wonderfully illustrated by the submissions for a recent Woodland Garden design competition.

In the autumn of every year *The Sunday Times* announces a garden design competition. Open to anyone, it always engenders a high degree of interest among amateur and young professional designers. Apart from cash awards, in the year following the competition announcement the first prizewinners have the joy of seeing their gardens built full-scale at the Chelsea Flower Show in May where they are viewed by more than a quarter of a million people. Occasionally, the designs of the runners-up are also built for the show and on one occasion the designs of all three prize-winners were given this valuable exposure which can do much for the prestige of designers at the beginning of their careers.

In addition, details of the winning designs are given prominent display in *The Sunday Times*, many of whose 4½ million readers are keenly interested in gardening. Thanks to their presence at the show and the interest of television, radio, magazine and newspaper journalists, several million more people throughout the world become aware of their achievement.

Making the prize-winning garden at Chelsea would not be possible without the co-operation of the Royal Horticultural Society which makes the much sought-after space available, and whose staff and officials always offer the practical help and advice necessary to ensure the best possible realisation of the winning design.

Despite all the brouhaha and publicity, the feature which most amazes and enchants the prize-winners is the pace at which in three weeks a patch of turf in the Royal Hospital Grounds in Chelsea is transformed into what is apparently a garden which has been established for years. This frequently includes the construction of highly elaborate buildings or features involving the placement of hundreds of tons of rock and the

planting of very large semi-mature trees with well-developed crowns and heights often in excess of 20 ft (6m). It is an achievement which depends upon a very close collaboration between *The Sunday Times* and a major professional garden contractor/nurseryman in partnership with other organisations willing to guarantee the supply on site at a particular time of the major materials necessary for the garden construction. The whole adds up to a piece of gardening theatre which for the participants provides the frenzy of hard work against the clock and the excitement of the ultimate achievement. There is little wonder that it usually makes the public who witness the results simply stand back and gasp. But visitors to *The Sunday Times* stand at the Chelsea Flower Show would be astonished almost equally by the designs submitted in the competition which the readers never see.

When launching the competition the aim was to try to stimulate public interest in better garden design, and certainly the standard of entries received in the decade during which the competition has been running suggests that there is no shortage of design talent or interest in the subject in Britain. Each year more than two thousand people usually apply for copies of the competition rules. Frequently and quite deliberately the brief which they receive is tight and exacting, the aim being usually either to seek designs which solve problems or to stimulate innovation.

Probably because the time available to prepare entries is fairly short (usually about eight weeks) and the competition rules are rigorous, only some 10 per cent of the people who bother to enquire about the competition actually submit entries, despite their best intentions. However, the standard of their submissions never fails to surprise the distinguished panel of judges drawn from a series of appropriate professional disciplines who are co-opted to adjudicate each year. They always conclude that practically all of the twenty or so designs left on the table for the final round of judging could be built at Chelsea without the reputation of *The Sunday Times* or the competition being in any way tarnished. Apart from the ingenuity displayed in the designs, what amazes the judges most is the remarkable talents which the entrants display in making their submissions attractive and interesting. As one judge put it:

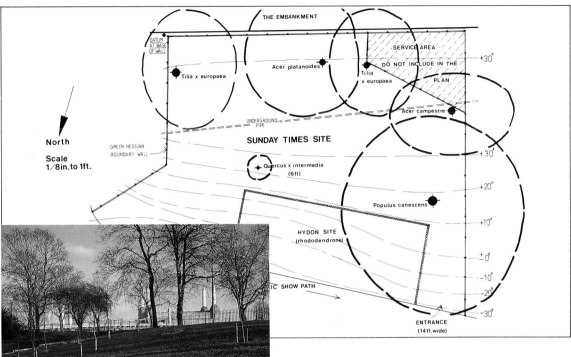

The site in the Royal Hospital grounds
in Chelsea which entrants to *The Sunday Times*
Woodland Garden design competition had to
transform.

'Some of them seem to write as well as Thoreau and draw as well as Leonardo.'

However, all the prize-winning designs are not as well presented. One man who has never won the competition but received awards in two of them made his submissions on scraps of rough paper on which he had drawn in ballpoint pen and which he had stuck on to card of the required size. He admitted that he was not very interested in gardening but had begun to sketch what he felt might be ideal gardens to distract himself while in hospital – and judging by his entries he is clearly a non-participant full of good gardening ideas.

He was not the only person without training as a landscaper to submit outstanding designs. Two major prizes have been won by an exhibition designer and a theatre designer; two others by architects whose professional work involves designing buildings and never gardens.

Sensing that because *The Sunday Times* only published details of the prize-winning designs and that they were being deprived of much potential pleasure over the years, perceptive readers (the directors of the publishers David & Charles among them) have frequently written to the paper asking if it would not be possible to offer them more.

When the Woodland Garden design competition was announced in October 1986, David & Charles took the initiative and suggested publishing something about it, including information about wildflower gardening which had been an important element in an earlier Wildlife Garden competition. Apart from providing the opportunity of exposing more than just the winning designs, David & Charles felt that it would provide a useful guide for anyone wishing to make a woodland and wildflower garden of their own. This book is the result – greatly enhanced by advice and illustrations from Alison Hainey, the winning designer. It is hoped that it might prove helpful to anyone whose garden is either hedged by or studded with largish trees who wished to exaggerate its woodland character or to anyone young enough and with sufficient courage and patience to be willing to make this charming form of garden from scratch on a bare site.

CHAPTER ONE

Elements of Good Woodland Gardens

In this lovely steep sided Welsh valley the over heavy top canopy of trees has been thinned by selective felling to provide better conditions for the establishment of a more varied tree and shrub planting.

Usually when announcing its garden design competition *The Sunday Times* publishes an article about the type of garden which is its subject. The aim is to provide potential entrants with a good example of the type of treatment required to fulfil the brief satisfactorily. Launching its Woodland Garden competition in October 1986, the paper drew attention to the work of the Kenaghan family in a remote corner of south-west Wales. Some of their achievements, while on a massive scale, could be emulated in a less ambitious way by anyone in just as short a time with even a much smaller garden provided that it was fringed by or contained a reasonable number of mature trees. Their experience, including the techniques which they developed for working on steep land and the mistakes which they made, is full of wonderful lessons for would-be woodland gardeners.

For many gardeners with sufficient land, their ideal would almost certainly be to re-create the atmosphere of a Le Douanier Rousseau painting. Dark and mysterious copses of bold foliage alternating with lighter, enchanting glades where blossoms predominate; the sort of environment where stumbling upon a leopard with emerald eyes while following a meandering track would come as no surprise.

If Jo Kenaghan has not yet contrived that degree of magic in her Post House Garden at Cwmbach, in Dyfed, its achievement cannot be long delayed. Meanwhile, in only ten years she has made one of the most delightful private woodland gardens in Britain.

No one who is familiar with the secret charms of the valley of the tiny Sien stream in this remote and beautiful corner of Wales could deny that its natural assets were perfect for the type of garden which Jo Kenaghan had in mind. Along with the house and responsibility of running the village post office, she and her husband bought 5 acres of the steep bank near the headwaters of the Sien. Her aim, she says, was to have boundless space to plant the rhododendrons and other flowering shrubs for which she has a passion and to ensure that her husband, a businessman, would have plenty to occupy him when he decides to retire. There is no doubt that she has achieved both objectives.

When the Kenaghans bought their valley side it was thickly overgrown with mounds of bramble beneath a dense canopy of seedling ash and sycamore, studded here and there with a few majestic oaks and the relics of elms killed by Dutch elm disease. In general, on the bank sides the soils are thin and acid but being so steeply sloped they drain well. However, on the flatter area where the house is sited with its foundations solidly fixed on a table of slate a foot or two below ground, the drainage is very poor indeed and this caused problems, as will be clear later. In many places access was difficult, because the land rose steeply from the stream's bank. As though to compensate for the problems which the stream creates, it gurgles melodiously; in its crystal water trout dart between the rocks and in late August svelte salmon wriggle their way over its low, stepped weirs.

It was the flat land nearest the house which Jo Kenaghan cleared first. After making a small lily pool, she planted fruit trees, tree peonies, lots of alpines and other herbaceous perennials, and some choice shrubs including what has become a handsome *Aralia elata* 'Aureovariegata', and some hybrid rhododendrons and camellias which she had moved from her former home.

Since such a large area of land was to become involved which would require hundreds of trees and shrubs if Jo Kenaghan was to make a significant impression, she knew that she would have to propagate and rear many of them herself. Because woodland gardens always require dense planting, debutant gardeners would also save themselves money by studying the techniques of raising trees and shrubs from seed and cuttings and by making the small initial investment in the necessary facilities. To be able to do her propagation, soon after her arrival Jo created a heated conservatory as a lean-to on one end of the house, built a group of frames in the yard behind and converted the relics of what had been the old watermill into a substantial cold house. Today, the first part of the garden beyond the buildings which has matured well and is not strictly tended, provides a lovely transition between the feeling of domesticity near the house and the wilder woodland garden further up the valley. But since it was the first section which Jo Kenaghan developed, it was here that she made her first important mistake. She did not take into account the change of climate between the Home Counties and south-west Wales. While her fruit trees have grown, for instance, they have not really prospered. Their limbs are badly cankered and the fruit frequently rots on the trees in the moist atmosphere. Nowadays, they simply provide a romantic background for the other plants.

Jo regrets not having realised that, apart from being damp, the area was a dangerous frost pocket and few of the choice collection of hybrid rhododendrons which she had planted initially have survived. 'I realise now that you must be aware of the features of the microclimate before planting anything precious.' As in any garden, her failures certainly stress the importance of considering rainfall, soil type, drainage, the disposition of the land in relation to the sun and the likelihood of heavy frosts before making decisions about which varieties to plant in a woodland garden because when competing hard for light, water and plant nutrients, as they will have to, plants must be appropriate to their site if they are to thrive.

After Jo Kenaghan's initial failures, she has successfully substituted much hardier species. Among the best are: *Rhododendron yakushimanum* (compact dome-shaped bushes with silvery young leaves and pale pink flowers); *R. fictolacteum* (a large shrub with bright cinnamon-felted young shoots and creamy-white crimson-blotched flowers); *R. arizelum* (a large shrub with magnificent large leaves and creamy yellow bell flowers); *R. haematodes* (a small bush with brilliant scarlet-crimson flowers), and *R. bureavii* (a medium-sized shrub with large tight trusses of pink bell-shaped crimson-marked flowers). They have all done well.

The more delicate sour green pea-like foliage of *Tropaeolum polyphyllum* tumbling down the steep bank behind the old mill contrasts splendidly with the dark green elephantine leaves of *Vitis cognetiae* as it climbs to provide an astonishing leaf-colour spectacular each autumn.

A pleasing jumble of shrub and hybrid tea roses flanks the left-hand side of the path leading from the house to the lily pond, which itself is surrounded by dwarf rhododendrons underplanted with variegated lily of the valley. Apart from the variegated aralia which is underplanted

with tree peonies, there are also conifers and a eucalyptus near the pool.

Poncirus trifoliata, some golden conifers, several more tree peonies, *Cornus contraversa* 'variegata', an *Embothrium*, *Elaeagnus commutata*, and many colours of *Hemerocallis* and *Alstroemeria* were chosen to parade in front of a rocky wall at the foot of the steep bankside.

A lesson which all gardeners could learn from Jo Kenaghan is to carry out the major earthworks at the outset and avoid having to damage established areas when making structural changes later. She hired a mechanical earth-mover and a driver who battled his way along the bank of the stream to the head of the valley, scoured out what had been a large pond and cut a streamside path coming back. This allowed access to the steep valley side where all the subsequent gardening has taken place. It involved cutting out the worst thickets of bramble and removing many of the poorer seedling trees to create lighter glades and allow the remaining trees to develop. This is an approach which beginners might overlook. If they own trees or tall shrubs which cast too much shadow over a particular area, by thoughtful pruning they can often thin a canopy selectively and overcome the problem without having to resort to the removal of the whole tree.

As each new area was cleared and the canopy thinned, Jo Kenaghan began her planting programme, respecting the main principle of woodland gardening which she believes is gently to enrich the wilderness with appropriate plants. She has planted thousands of trees, shrubs and herbaceous plants which will prosper in Cwmbach's thin and acid shaly soil. Many of the ashes, blackthorns, sycamores and brambles have been replaced by rowans, laburnums and ornamental malus and prunus species.

There are many notable features on the low walk along the riverside path encountered between the house area and the large upper millpond (which used to be the reservoir for the watermill), and we describe them here in sequence (see plan on page 16).

To the left of the path, more hardy rhododendrons and camellias underplanted with Welsh poppies and Trilliums with fine examples of *Sanguinaria canadensis pleno*.

To the right, a charming rose arbour surrounded by a planting of acers, rhododendrons, magnolias, camellias underplanted with peonies, many varieties of hosta, anemones and wild orchids. The ground here is a solid carpet of snowdrops in early spring.

To the left, rhododendron hybrids below an old quarry devoted to rhododendron species.

To the right, half-way along the path to the large pond, there is a small wooden building flanked by a small garden with a patch of mown lawn, roses and shrubs. A store and base camp for work on the slopes, it serves as an area for tranquil riverside repose and picnic teas.

To the left, on the lower slopes of the bank running down to the large pond, parrotias, liquid amber and Exbury azaleas flourish, and the ground is covered with bluebells in the spring.

Around the pond and the steps leading to the upper path there are more rhododendrons raised from seed, clematis, crinodendrons, old shrub and climbing roses (mounting trees) and a dazzling *Lirodendron tulipifera* 'Aureo marginatum'.

Turning right when reaching the upper path and then right again down some steps, there is a bog garden being formed in the damp bed of what was a reserve mill-pond. Here willows, hostas, *Ligularias*, *Rodgersias*, primulas and *Mecanopsis napaulensis* thrive.

On the journey back down the valley on the upper path, to create added interest in cleared areas of the woodland, Jo Kenaghan, with the aid of her husband and children, has planted a wide range of azaleas, rhododendrons and camellia species and hybrids. After her early failures with rhododendrons, however, she has selected the hardier hybrids like the white Polar Bear, Pink Pearl, the yellow Hawk Crest, and the red Jean Mary Montague. All of these tend to be late-flowering and escape frost damage.

Late-flowering magnolias like *Magnolia watsonii* and *M. wilsonii*, maples, viburnums and parrotias also add variety to the woodland. Many herbaceous plants like peonies, Solomon's seal,

ferns, hostas and trilliums have developed into thriving clumps at their feet to join with hosts of wildflowers like bluebells and meadowsweet to offer a parade of colour throughout the season.

Additional interest in this area is offered by moutain ash and whitebeams, malus and fruit trees in variety grown as much for their blossom and the colour and shape of their fruit as for their crops. Jo Kenaghan has also managed to make the whole area retain a very natural appearance by resisting the temptation to include too many of the more exquisite and highly ornamental species in each area. This means that when beauties like the small tree *Amelanchier canadensis* do appear, their star quality is instantly recognised and the more greatly enjoyed. This is also a feature of the way in which she has established swatches of primulas and fat clumps of *Romneya coulteri* among the general underbrush.

They can all be enjoyed by visitors when

Large rough cut slate slabs (above) make an attractive margin for the lily pool in Jo Kenaghan's woodland garden. Simple structures like this rustic plank and pole bridge (above right) look best in woodland situations.
Very pale or rather vivid colours such as those seen here (right) always contrast well with the generally dark backgrounds in a woodland. Note how the distant rhododendron beckons for attention leading the eye along the mown grass path.

walking along the thousands of yards of contour paths around the hillside. The paths are linked between levels by flights of meandering rustic steps made from timber cut during the woodland thinning. This timber has also been used to make many welcome seats from which the general woodscape can be enjoyed, or the ducks watched on the pond.

Even if new woodland gardeners cannot obtain logs on their own land in order to follow the Kenaghans' example in making appropriately rustic steps or seats or using them to hold back the outer edges of paths across sloping land, rough timber is usually obtainable at the sawmills of the many forestry enterprises which exist in all parts of the country. These firms also frequently offer good timber fencing, gates, etc.

Not far from the house, a branch from the upper path leads down to a favoured area where Jo Kenaghan has established her rhododendron

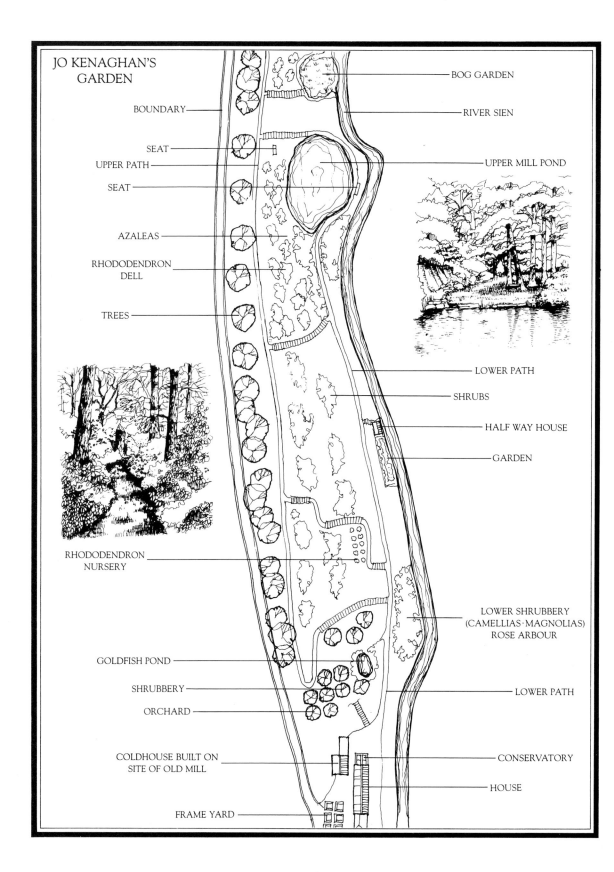

JO KENAGHAN'S GARDEN

BOUNDARY

SEAT

UPPER PATH

SEAT

AZALEAS

RHODODENDRON DELL

TREES

RHODODENDRON NURSERY

GOLDFISH POND

SHRUBBERY

ORCHARD

COLDHOUSE BUILT ON SITE OF OLD MILL

FRAME YARD

BOG GARDEN

RIVER SIEN

UPPER MILL POND

LOWER PATH

SHRUBS

HALF WAY HOUSE

GARDEN

LOWER SHRUBBERY (CAMELLIAS·MAGNOLIAS) ROSE ARBOUR

LOWER PATH

CONSERVATORY

HOUSE

nursery where she lines out to grow on seedlings which she has produced under glass and in her frames. She now has over one hundred of her own unnamed seedlings established as the result of her having collected seed from the hundred different named hybrids and species which she has imported.

Just before reaching the final flight of steps from the upper path back down to the house, she has abandoned all restraint, contriving a plant spectacular to send her visitors away reeling from the pageant of form and colour which they have been offered. *Davidia involucrata, Cornus kousa, Cercis siliquastrum, Eucryphia, Camellia, Enkianthus, Exochorda, Kalmia, Mahonia*, and more roses and herbaceous plants all jostle merrily for attention.

Jo Kenaghan is aware that a tract of undisturbed woodland can be pretty but that it is a wilderness and not a garden. Usually in any area, although it might be beautiful by moments, it will be too dominated by a few aggressive species to offer season-long interest to gardeners. Wandering through hundreds of acres of woodland, they would certainly pass through many sufficiently diverse ecological niches, each with its own dominant species, to offer satisfying variety; but that is serious forest walking, not garden strolling which takes place over much smaller patches of ground. Like all good woodland gardeners, therefore, Jo Kenaghan has seen her role as someone who gently tinkers with nature, curbing its aggressions and inseminating the wild with more ornamental species which look appropriate in a woodland setting. She conceives a good woodland garden as being something just as artificial and contrived as every other sort of garden, but she contends that its plan should never be obvious and it should retain a very natural look. That is why her garden never looks too interfered with and well groomed. Unless they threaten the establishment of the plants which she has introduced or threaten to become too dominant, she makes little attempt to quell the development of weeds, many of which are beautiful wildflowers

which contribute their own charm to the whole scheme.

Her approach to planning was that which should be adopted by all woodland gardeners. She thinned the top canopy and the underbrush in places where it had become too dense and made access difficult, then considered what assets each area had to offer. She allowed the form and disposition of the land itself to suggest how it should be best developed rather than merely drawing a plan on paper and deciding where everything should be situated.

This was particularly important on her steeply sloping site where the contours are close and the actual land surface available for planting is much greater than it appears in two dimensions on paper. As her garden has evolved, its possibilities for development have increased. 'Until the bog garden was established there was no particular reason to make a seat from which it could be overlooked,' she pointed out, 'and until an area of land is cleared you don't realise that there is a gentle undulation which might make a cosy home for a plant which is intolerant of wind.' Similarly, as plantings develop in places the original thinning may prove to be inadequate and such factors should constantly be reappraised. It may be necessary to do more selective pruning of the canopy to make 'windows' which allow particularly beautiful plants to be seen more clearly and lure the eye down vistas which will help to give form to the garden and its various areas in a way which seems logical and satisfying.

Finally, Jo Kenaghan offers two practical tips to anyone setting out to create a woodland garden. Even though a nondescript tree which has been badly damaged in past storms might commend itself as a suitable subject for treatment with the chain saw, the gardener should think twice before deciding that it should be felled because it might make a very attractive climbing frame for something as exquisite as a *species clematis* or as romantic as an ivy. If it is finally felled, all the useful timber should be saved to make steps, seats or retaining walls for the outer edges of paths along steep slopes, and all the twigs and remaining smaller branches should be shredded and mixed with fallen leaves to make a compost for mulching around newly planted trees and shrubs both to help to feed them and keep down weeds.

The garden seems very narrow in plan but because it slopes very steeply from the river margin on the right up to the boundary on the left it is really very extensive with room for thousands of shrubs and trees.

CHAPTER TWO

Making the
Chelsea Garden

20 days before this photograph was taken the land was just a
bare grassy bank overhung by a few tall trees.

A garden at the Chelsea Flower Show which the public could stroll through casually to enjoy its detail had long been a cherished notion of *Sunday Times Magazine* editor Philip Clarke. He imagined it as being an area of calm and large enough for visitors to feel that they were an important part of the garden while able to forget that the crowded show avenues and buzzing central London were but minutes away.

It needed really big trees to be effective, he emphasised, frequently standing to tower over his desk and lift his arms towards the ceiling and swing them back down to his sides to mime the canopy of a forest giant. And it had to have everything, he insisted. There must be water, marshy areas, flower-studded meadow lawns, smooth mown turf, a wonderful informal parade of colour from herbaceous plants and shrubs alike. Vistas, too, with statuary to lure the eye would be a feature as would a fragrant pergola through which visitors could pass. And like all the best gardens there would have to be a charming loggia from which it could be enjoyed, no matter how chilly the wind or even if it was raining. That is how, in 1984, the idea of a Woodland Garden design competition for the Chelsea Show was born.

When approached about the idea, the Royal Horticultural Society was immediately sympathetic and promised to consider ways in which such a large garden could be accommodated on the limited land available for the garden displays. But no matter how the show officials manoeuvred with their rulers, set squares and compasses on the showground plan, for the next two years they could not resolve what was essentially a problem of geometry. There simply was not enough room on land which could easily be viewed from the avenues where visitors walked to offer any exhibitor a bigger frontage than that normally required, without being unfair to their fellow exhibitors who also had intriguing gardens to display. Had there been any way of making more avenue frontage available, there was a long waiting list of potential garden exhibitors anxious to benefit from the situation.

Then, early in 1986, someone had a good idea. At the eastern end of what is known as the embankment site in the grounds of the Royal Hospital at Chelsea, the show committee always left a very generous area of the fairly steep bankside free of exhibits so that visitors could use it for their picnics on fine days. It was felt that without too much hardship for the public a portion of that land could be added to the display space. When considering that possibility, it became clear that anyone occupying that space would have ready access to a large area of land which normally remained hidden behind an area on which for several years the famous Hydon Nurseries had displayed its dazzling rhododendrons. At most previous shows this hidden land had been used by Hydon and other embankment site exhibitors to store their equipment, plants and materials while preparing their displays. If Hydon Nurseries could be persuaded to share a storage area further back on the southern margin of the embankment site and *The Sunday Times* could be given small exit and entrance frontages on either side of the Hydon display, there would be enough land behind to make a large garden of the type envisaged. Without hesitation, Hydon Nurseries not only agreed to the plan but offered to landscape the edges of its display with rhododendrons and azaleas placed informally so that anybody walking in a garden behind would think that it was just a splendid rhododendron thicket on its northern edge. With this collaboration ensured and the blessing of the RHS show committee, it was possible to announce the Woodland Garden design competition in the autumn of 1986 and build the winning garden for display at the 1987 Chelsea Flower Show.

When the English Gardening School at the Chelsea Physic Garden turned in their carefully surveyed plan of the heavily contoured site for the competition garden, it was clear that one of Philip Clarke's requirements would certainly be met. Several very large trees would overhang much of the garden, providing the type of high canopy which every really satisfactory woodland garden possesses. It was obvious, too, that although the site had rather an odd shape, with a large rectangular bite taken out of its northern boundary, if the designer was facing a real, rather than a flower show, situation, that rectangle of land might well be occupied by the client's house (see plan of site on page 9).

The two shortish lengths of frontage on to the

southern avenue of the show would, it was realised, be an advantage rather than a disadvantage, allowing visitors to enter the garden on one side and leave it through the other. With the vast crowds which turn up at Chelsea, the possibility of contriving a smooth flow through the garden was a considerable asset.

When potential entrants responded to the competition launch by writing for the rules, they were told that a suitable footpath was a compulsory feature. Among the mandatory features (see Appendix for the rules in full) were a tranquil sitting and viewing loggia, a pond, several semi-mature trees and large shrubs, drifts of nominated appropriate wildflowers, entrance and exit gateways and surround fencing.

To turn a patch of Chelsea turf into a garden in three weeks requires a command of logistics similar to that possessed by the generals who planned and co-ordinated all the services for the landing on the Normandy beaches. Even before the competition was announced, Michael Miller, Managing Director of London's Clifton Nurseries, was co-opted as the operation commander who, with his

landscape contracts manager Chris Bowles, would turn the competition winner's dream into a reality. He, in his turn, needed the co-operation of organisations like the quarrymen Marshalls Mono of Halifax who would guarantee to deliver stone needed for walling and paving in the right grades and quantities on site to meet a precise schedule. Similar promises were obtained from Breedon and Cloud Hill Limeworks of Derby for the delivery of tons of its gravel to top pathways and Cambark Products of Cambridge for the copious loads of its wood bark products used to clad the ground in the planted areas.

Since many large shrubs and semi-mature trees would be required to make the garden, Miller and his staff scoured the country's specialist nurseries to obtain promises that sufficient would be reserved and prepared and delivered on time for planting at Chelsea in the following May. Arrangements were made at the same time for the supply of the hundreds of appropriate garden herbaceous plants like foxgloves, lilies and bergenias to be available after forcing in heated glasshouses or being held back in cool stores so that as

By allowing the ends of two small ponds to disappear below the margins of a bridge structure laid out over solid ground visitors to the Chelsea garden were convinced that they were crossing quite a large pond.

many as possible of them would be in flower, for while all the plants which the winning design called for could not be anticipated and ordered in advance, production of a great many of the likely nominations had to be got underway.

Because they had been listed as compulsory ingredients in the garden, the wildflowers were less of a problem. The list had been drawn up by the Institute of Terrestrial Ecology which has gained a fine reputation for both wildflower study, advice and production. With the collaboration of specialist wildflower seed supplier John Chambers of Kettering, Dr Laurie Boorman, Alan Frost and their colleagues at the Institute's headquarters at Abbots Ripton, near Huntingdon, agreed to rear a fine selection of typical woodland and woodland margin wildflowers.

All these preliminary arrangements had been made before Alison Hainey and her fellow competition entrants had even begun to stew over its rules and formulate their ideas on how to tackle the site. Alison was 30 at the time. After a thorough training in landscape architecture at Manchester Polytechnic, she had extended her experience abroad by working for spells in Philadelphia, USA, and Hong Kong before settling in London to work for a firm of architects. She had been contemplating a landscaping practice of her own when she saw the competition announcement. She was attracted to it because visitors would be able to walk through the garden, and that is in accord with her views about landscaping which she feels 'should relate to people'. She also felt that if she did well in the competition it would attract attention to her work and perhaps lead to commissions which would help to support a young practice.

Alison conceived her garden (see overleaf for plans) as being either an informal part of a large country garden in which it might be surrounded by more formal areas or as a complete suburban garden with formal gardens attached to houses on either side. That is why when placing its entrance at the western end of the plot she chose to make a pergola 'swathed in clouds of white wisteria', its first dramatic feature which she felt would make 'an effective transition between the comparative formality of the surrounding gardens and the secrets of the woodland garden'. She understood that moving from an open and bright

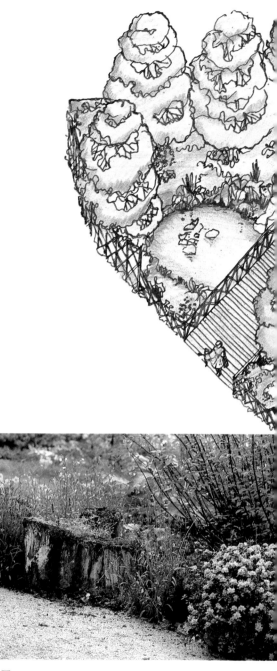

Even at the early planning stage Alison Hainey had begun to consider the inclusion of telling details in her competition garden. But even she could not have anticipated that they would be as charmingly interpreted as they were by Cliftons Nurseries at Chelsea. The picture above shows a typical treatment of a path edge. Its margins have been blurred by an overhang of azalea and the inclusion of a beautifully weathered old stone trough.

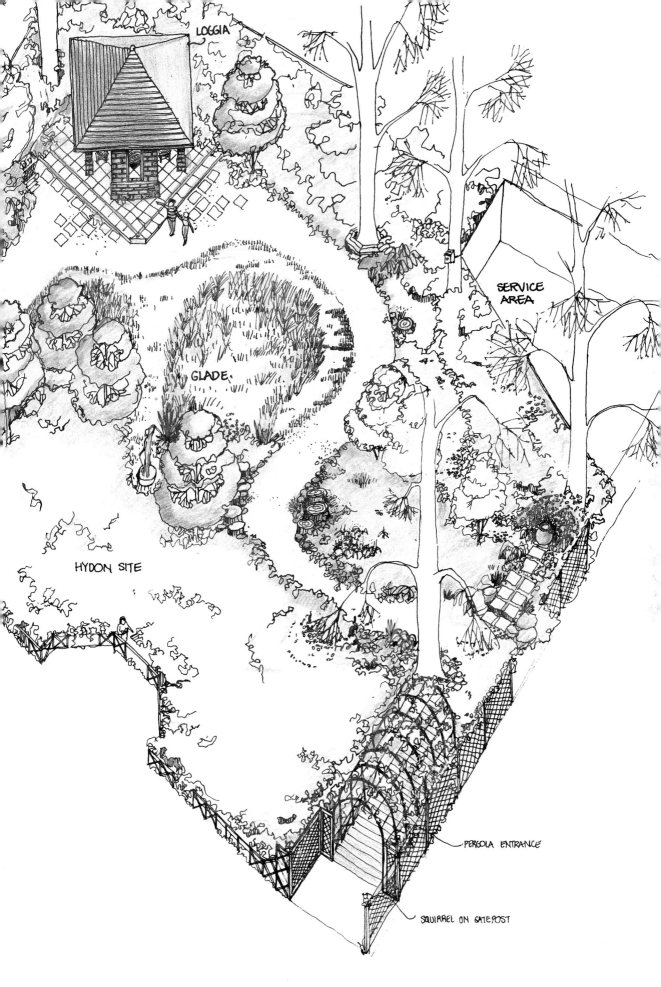

LOGGIA

SERVICE
AREA

GLADE

HYDON SITE

PERGOLA ENTRANCE

SQUIRREL ON GATEPOST

PLANTING PLAN

1. *Acer japonicum* 'Aureum'
2. *Acer negundo*
3. *Acer palmatum* 'Atropurpureum'
4. *Acer palmatum* 'Dissectum Atropurpureum'
5. *Acer palmatum* 'Dissectum Viridis'
6. *Ajuga reptans*
7. *Alchemilla mollis*
8. *Allium ursinum*
9. *Arundinaria nitida*
10. *Asperula odorata*
11. *Astilbe* 'Ceres'
12. *Astilbe × arendsii* 'Bridal Veil'
13. *Athyrium filix-femina*
14. *Azalea* 'Balzac'
15. *Azalea* 'Daviesii'
16. *Azalea* 'Gog'
17. *Azalea* 'Golden Horn'
18. *Azalea* 'Mikado'
19. *Berberis candidula*
20. *Bergenia in variety*
21. *Betula pendula* 'Youngii'
22. *Buddleia alternifolia*
23. *Buxus sempervirens*
24. *Caltha palustris*
25. *Cardamine pratensis*
26. *Carex flacca*
27. *Ceanothus dentatus*
28. *Ceanothus thyrsiflorus repens*
29. *Convallaria majalis*
30. *Cornus alba* 'Aurea'
31. *Cornus alba* 'Sibirica'
32. *Cotoneaster conspicuus* 'Decorus'
33. *Cotoneaster dammeri*
34. *Cotoneaster horizontalis*
35. *Cotoneaster × watereri*
36. *Cytisus* 'Donard Seedling'
37. *Cytisus purpureus*
38. *Digitalis* 'Excelsior' hybrids
39. *Enkianthus campanulatus*
40. *Euonymus* 'Emerald Cushion'
41. *Euonymus* 'Emerald Gaiety'
42. *Euphorbia polychroma*
43. *Genista pilosa*
44. *Geranium pratense*
45. *Hedera* 'Pittsburg'
46. *Hedera* 'Brigette'
47. *Hedera* 'Ingelise'
48. *Hedera* 'Mona Lisa'
49. *Hedera* 'Montgomery'
50. *Hosta fortunei*
51. *Hosta fortunei* 'Albopicta'
52. *Hosta glauca*
53. *Hosta sieboldiana* 'Frances Williams'
54. *Hosta* 'Thomas Hogg'
55. *Hosta undulata*
56. *Hosta undulata erromena*
57. *Hyacinthoides non-scripta*
58. *Ilex aquifolium* 'J. C. van Tol'
59. *Iris pseudacorus*
60. *Lamium galeobdolon*
61. *Leucanthemum vulgare*
62. *Lilium regale*
63. *Lonicera serotina*
64. *Lunaria annua* 'Variegata Alba'
65. *Lychnis flos-cuculi*
66. *Lysimachia vulgaris*
67. *Lythrum salicaria*
68. *Macleaya cordata*
69. *Mahonia japonica*
70. *Mahonia lomariifolia*
71. *Matteuccia struthiopteris*
72. *Nicotiana affinis*
73. *Pieris* 'Forest Flame'
74. *Pieris japonica*
75. *Pieris japonica variegata*
76. *Pieris taiwanensis*
77. *Pinus mugo* 'Gnom'
78. *Pinus nigra*
79. *Pinus sylvestris*
80. *Primula veris*
81. *Primula vulgaris*
82. *Prunus lusitanica*
83. *Pulmonaria* 'Munstead Blue'
84. *Rheum palmatum*
85. *Rheum tanguticum*
86. *Rheum palimaturis*
87. *Rhododendron* 'Catawbiense Boursault'
88. *Rhododendron* 'Catawbiense Grandiflorum'
89. *Rhododendron* 'Cynthia'
90. *Rhododendron* 'Engl. Roseum'

91. *Rhododendron* 'Fastuosum Flore Pleno'
92. *Rhododendron* 'Goldfort'
93. *Rhododendron* 'Lady Clementine Milford'
94. *Rhododendron* 'Lady Primrose'
95. *Rhododendron* 'Miss R. S. Holford'
96. *Rhododendron* 'Mother of Pearl'
97. *Rhododendron* 'Mrs Charles Pearson'
98. *Rhododendron* 'Mrs W. C. Slocock'

99. *Rhododendron naomi* 'Stella Maris'
100. *Rhododendron* Pink Hybrid
101. *Rhododendron* Yellow Hybrid
102. *Rosa canina*
103. *Rosa* 'Iceberg'
104. *Rosa* 'Albertine'
105. *Rosa* 'Coral Dawn'
106. *Rosa* 'Madame Alfred Carriere'
107. *Rosa* 'Handel'
108. *Rosa* 'Swan Lake'

EXISTING TREES

PROPOSED TREES

SHRUBS

WILDFLOWERS

MOWN GRASS

MEADOW LAND

GRAVEL PATH

BARK MULCH PATH

TIMBER LOG FEATURE

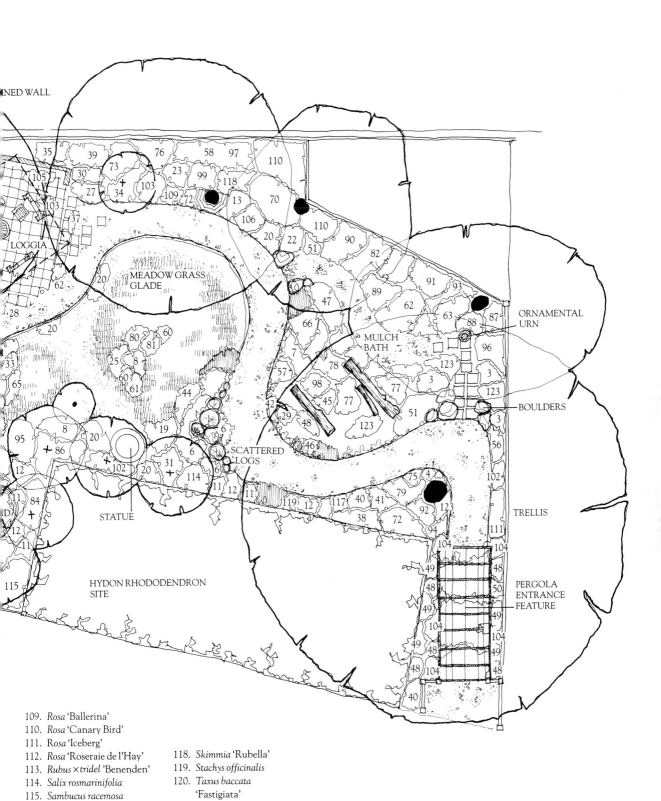

NED WALL

35   39   76   58   97

73   23   110

105   30   99   118

27   34   103   109 72   13   70

103   37   106

LOGGIA   20   22   110

62   51   90

20   MEADOW GRASS GLADE   82

28   89   91   93

20   47   62   63   88   87   ORNAMENTAL URN

33   66   MULCH BATH   96

65   80   60   78   123   3

81   25   8   57   98   77   123

60   61   45   77   51   BOULDERS

44   42   29   48   123   3

95   8   20   19   46   56

86   102   6   SCATTERED LOGS   75   4   102

12   31   20   114   79   123   TRELLIS

11   84   11   12   11   119   12   117   40   41   92   123   111

D   STATUE   38   72   94

12   104

11   49   48

115   HYDON RHODODENDRON SITE   48   50   PERGOLA ENTRANCE FEATURE

49   104

104   49

49   48   104   48

40

area through the constriction of an attractive and fragrant tunnel in which the light is subdued and tinted green when filtering through a thick canopy of foliage, and then emerging to another bright and open area, can have a marked effect on the perceptions. Slightly baffling, the passage through the pergola seems to dim images registered before entering the tunnel. This makes the brighter light and new views registered beyond its exit always seem to come as a surprise.

To ensure that visitors would be lured on through the pergola she immediately earmarked their attention by attracting their eyes right to the southern margin of the garden, initially down the beginning of the main gravel path and then beyond, along stepping-stones through a shrubbery, to a large ornamental earthenware pot. Gently curving and mounting the contours of the sloping site, the main gravel path would take visitors high into the garden and then wend back down to the eastern exit, passing the loggia and crossing the pond en route. Deep in the woodland, in the filtered light breaking through the high canopy, bluebells, periwinkles, lily of the valley, dogwood and wood sorrel were selected to shine out against typical natural woodland shrubs such as hazel, dog rose and elder. The greater light intensity in the glade allowed the inclusion on the plan of a flower meadow composed of grasses and

A flower meadow like that shown above makes a perfect soft floor for an open woodland glade while astilbes massed into large drifts shine out wonderfully from the shadow beneath trees.
A scattering of characterful boulders and an attractive stone vase (right) act as wonderful foils for the flowers and foliage of rhododendrons, foxgloves and hostas in this most successful corner of the Chelsea garden.

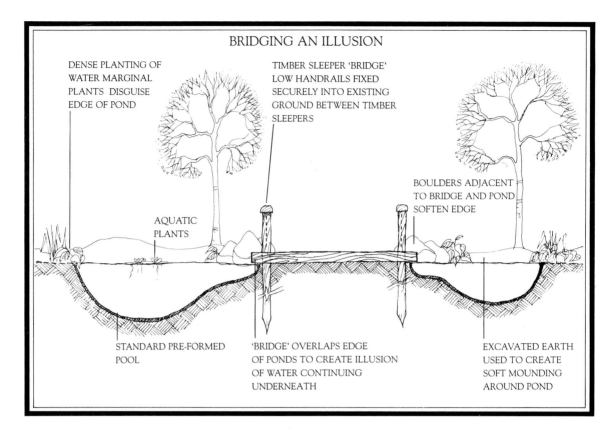

BRIDGING AN ILLUSION

DENSE PLANTING OF WATER MARGINAL PLANTS DISGUISE EDGE OF POND

TIMBER SLEEPER 'BRIDGE' LOW HANDRAILS FIXED SECURELY INTO EXISTING GROUND BETWEEN TIMBER SLEEPERS

AQUATIC PLANTS

BOULDERS ADJACENT TO BRIDGE AND POND SOFTEN EDGE

STANDARD PRE-FORMED POOL

'BRIDGE' OVERLAPS EDGE OF PONDS TO CREATE ILLUSION OF WATER CONTINUING UNDERNEATH

EXCAVATED EARTH USED TO CREATE SOFT MOUNDING AROUND POND

wildflowers and a wider variety of herbaceous plants to be established. At the edge of the meadow ornamental rhubarb was nominated to 'rub shoulders with spiky foxtail lilies and Californian poppies'.

At the path sides, piles of randomly arranged logs were designed to provide a haven for wood-boring insects, a growing ground for mosses and liverworts and a happy niche in whose shelter 'woodland floor primroses, anemones and wild strawberries could flourish'. A majestic old lime tree which existed on the site was chosen to shade a cunningly planned, shingle-roofed, open-sided loggia with stone walls to baffle any wind, and windows to offer all-round views.

More domestic plants such as mahonias and viburnums which have strong architectural qualities, and clay pots and urns filled with an assortment of blue, white and yellow flowering annuals, were to be planted in the immediate vicinity and stationed on the terrace to offer gardeners a chance to show off their talents. It was suggested that in the cool of the evening gardeners could relax in the loggia and enjoy the drift of

perfumed scent from the flower meadow while admiring the dazzling blue and white woodland carpet or the dramatic planting which would frame the pond below. This was envisaged surrounded by the luxuriant and eye-catching flowers of marsh-loving plants with the erect grasses and sword-leaved irises contrasting with the horizontal floating water-lily pads and the umbrella-leafed *Gunnera* and cabbage-leaved bog arum.

These nuances would be best appreciated from a simple wooden bridge crossing the middle of the pond designed to offer the opportunity of peering into its depths and enjoying the sensation of being suspended in space, which is always part of the fascination of crossing any bridge.

Other thoughtful and appealing features which Alison Hainey included in her design were:

🌿Paths mown through the grass in both the meadow-lawn and more heavily wooded areas offering alternative intriguing routes with other vistas including, at the end of one path, an eye-catching sculpture.

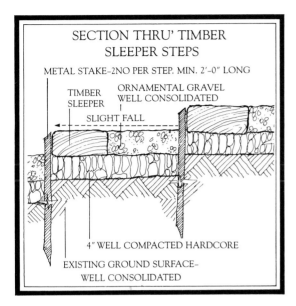

SECTION THRU' TIMBER
SLEEPER STEPS

METAL STAKE–2NO PER STEP. MIN. 2'-0" LONG

TIMBER
SLEEPER

ORNAMENTAL GRAVEL
WELL CONSOLIDATED

SLIGHT FALL

4" WELL COMPACTED HARDCORE

EXISTING GROUND SURFACE–
WELL CONSOLIDATED

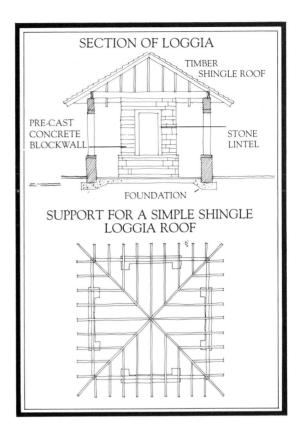

SECTION OF LOGGIA

TIMBER
SHINGLE ROOF

PRE-CAST
CONCRETE
BLOCKWALL

STONE
LINTEL

FOUNDATION

SUPPORT FOR A SIMPLE SHINGLE
LOGGIA ROOF

Good steps in woodland paths (above) look the most natural if they are kept informal with stout wooden risers holding back treads of well consolidated gravel. Timber sleepers (left) laid on a mound of earth between railings flanked by ponds excavated to below the sleeper margins will give the impression that a bridge spans a large pond.

A timber octagonal seat around the trunk of a tree alongside the gravel path.

A nesting-box high on the trunk of one of the more secluded trees.

A simulated ruined wall behind the loggia to support colourful trailing plants and ivy.

Early in January 1987 the competition entries were judged by television gardener Peter Seabrook; Laurie Boorman of the Institute of Terrestrial Ecology; Harry Hartley, Marketing Director, Marshalls Mono Ltd; Arthur George, Managing Director, Hydon Nurseries Ltd; Rosemary Alexander, Principal, The English Gardening School, and Michael Miller, Managing Director of Clifton Nurseries Ltd. Against stiff competition from the entries of the designers who were awarded the other prizes or whose designs were highly commended and commended, Alison Hainey's design was selected as the winner, because, the judges stated afterwards, 'it most cleverly combined the compulsory features with

the whole concept of creating a woodland garden so that the wildflowers blend in with and enhance the natural woodland atmosphere'. They were clearly most impressed by Alison Hainey's original, stylish yet appropriately rustic approach to the design of the loggia, her simple rather poetic interpretation of the brief and the great sensitivity of her suggested planting scheme.

After heavily grazing the buffet tables and expressing their satisfaction in an interesting morning's work well done and their eager anticipation of seeing the design built at Chelsea, most of the judges left Michael Miller poring over Alison's drawings. It was his job to make the design a reality and he was anxious to examine again her detailed planting lists. Apart from the location of the plants listed as compulsory ingredients in the garden, he wanted to know how many of her free selections he had anticipated. He knew that it would be unlikely that he could obtain all the plants which she had nominated in sufficient quantities or in a suitable state of growth to be able to include them in the Chelsea garden, but he wanted to try to satisfy her requirements as

The before and after pictures above reveal the Chelsea showman's trick of creating gravel paths between wooden edging fixed above the general level of the ground. It is a technique which could be very useful in ill drained sections of any garden.

These pictures (left and above) show two stages in the creation of the shallow flight of steps leading down from the loggia to the bridge over the pond. Note how really robust timber risers have been used to hold back the gravel infill of the treads.

To produce the instant effect which is demanded of a successful Chelsea garden large quantities of plants at an attractive stage of growth are necessary. But having got them onto the site a good deal of thought is necessary before they are finally nestled into place. Here Chris Bowles (above on left) and Michael Miller (centre) discuss a home for some hostas.

Short stakes (left) are now considered the most satisfactory for securing semi-mature trees after planting.

far as possible, and whenever it was obvious that something would be too difficult to obtain he had to try to suggest a suitable alternative which was more readily available.

Some time after his fellow judges had gone home he picked up Alison's design and, muttering that he wished he had had two seasons' warning of what would be needed, he left *The Sunday Times Magazine* offices in Gray's Inn Road.

The sequence in which the professionals, Cliftons, tackled the work of turning the Chelsea site into a garden in three weeks provides a wonderful example to amateurs of the way in which they, too, should proceed. Amateurs so frequently paint themselves into corners by bad planning. Anxious to obtain long dreamt of effects, they plant and tidy areas of their gardens before realising that, because heavy barrowing or machines are involved, the next major project on the site is likely to completely ravage their previous good work. Firms like Cliftons avoid such traumas by spending a considerable time on studying the logistics of the operation. This even goes as far as deciding exactly where on the site heavy materials should be off-loaded so that they will be as close as possible to the area in which they are to be used and therefore require a minimum of subsequent handling. It is important, too, that the materials should be available immediately that they are needed and not be dumped where their presence will make other operations difficult.

Cliftons made sure that all the major civil engineering and building was completed before a single plant was introduced. A mechanical digger was used to excavate trenches for the concrete foundations of the folly wall behind the loggia, the loggia walls and the cavities to take the pond liners. Before leaving the site, it was used to scrape flat a horizontal area for the loggia terrace and to gently grade the entrance slope beneath the future pergola and to help to cut steps to make negotiating the bank between the loggia and the exit bridge easier. Some of the planting holes to take the larger trees and shrubs were also dug by the machine before it was sent away.

Since most of the concrete and cement would be required in the loggia area, the sand, aggregate, cement and cement mixer were also stationed there, as were the stone blocks and paving slabs. The day after the foundations had been poured, loggia building began. When its walls had reached the level of the eaves and were ready to take the roof timbers, its floor and the immediate area outside the walls were paved.

While the roof timbers were created by the carpenters on site and clad in the board to which the shingles were attached, the simulated bridge was created at the eastern exit. This involved making a humped mound of earth and covering it with heavy timbers. It may seem a strange way to make a bridge, but it is a very satisfactory trick which gardeners could easily copy. Instead of making a single pond with a continuous stretch of water flowing beneath the bridge, Cliftons made two smaller ponds with the simulated bridge set between them. The plastic pond liners used fitted snugly into the side of the 'bridge' mound so that, when peering over the bridge rail visitors looked straight down into water. Clever planting in and on the edge of the ponds at the points where they met the bridge mound gave the impression that it was genuine when it was seen from elsewhere in the garden. This blatant deception meant that a costly bridge well engineered to carry large crowds did not have to be built.

Something which most visitors to the Chelsea Flower Show do not perhaps appreciate is that most of the buildings and walls that they see are not jerry-built shams only designed to remain sound for the four-day duration of the show. Both the loggia and the simulated bridge in the woodland garden were made to normal building and landscaping standards. Had they not been broken up and fully demolished (including the concrete wall foundations) on the Saturday after the show closed, they would have been capable of gracing the Royal Hospital grounds for decades.

While the work on those structures was under way, more of Cliftons' landscaping staff were erecting the tubular steel pergola arches which were specially made because the standard arches available would not have been wide enough to span a pathway to take the crowds expected in the

Very mature looking planting around a pool which is less than 24 hours old demonstrates the attractive effect which can be obtained by ensuring that in each area there is a mix of vegetation of such different character as that of the fluffy headed cream astilbes and the succulent kingcups.

show. When they were in place, trellis panels were put up to flank them. It is as well to observe here that although Alison Hainey had her vision of a thirty-year-old white wisteria festooning the pergola so that its metal structure would have vanished beneath a wrapping of aged stems and abundant foliage, she was wise enough to realise that when first put up, no pergola could look like that. So she wisely specified the flanking trellis work to increase the sense of enclosure when moving through the pergola and to offset some of its new metallic bleakness.

When making the gravel path, Cliftons used a trick which old show hands often employ but some amateur path-makers might find appealing for other reasons. Clearing the site after the show can be a time-consuming and costly business. To avoid this, many contractors build their paths on top of firmly consolidated ground. They prefer to do this rather than excavate, because after excavation it is necessary to find somewhere off the garden site to temporarily tip the earth and moving to and from the dump involves two unnecessary operations. Once the soil has been disturbed, considerable efforts are required to level its bed to make a smooth path. It is also more difficult to remove all the hardcore and gravel used to make the path when the show is over.

At Chelsea, Cliftons first used long strips of thin, flexible, plywood 5 in (13 cm) wide to define the path edges, holding them upright between stout wooden pegs driven firmly into the turf. Black polythene sheeting was then laid into the bottom and up the sides of the shallow trough formed between these wooden edges before it was filled with 'as dug' (unwashed) gravel which was well compacted with a vibrating roller. Left in that state, standing 5 in (12.5 cm) proud of the surrounding ground, the path would have looked rather bizarre, but the appearance was soon changed by using a peaty loam mixture to raise gently the level of the surrounding ground to the top of the outside edge of the wood holding the gravel in place. Fresh turf was used at Chelsea to cover these mini earthworks rapidly as it could be in a garden. However, in a garden it would be equally appropriate to sow the loam with grass or, as at Chelsea, to use some of it to provide a home for creeping plants whose stems and foliage helped to blur the harshness of the path edges.

A random pile of cut and split logs and an old woodmans axe make it seem that he has just finished work for the day. Apart from making good shelters for plants like primroses and violets, features like this impart authenticity to a woodland garden.

The advantage of this technique to a show contractor is that if he is careful he can use a machine at the end of the show to remove most of the gravel and easily collect the residue by lifting short lengths of the sheet plastic and taking the gravel with it. Gardeners might consider making paths in this way if excavation with the problem of dumping the spoil is undesirable or impossible because buried pipes or cables might be encountered. Since to be really useful paths should drain and dry out quickly in wet weather in this respect, paths built above the general ground level always have an advantage over excavated paths, and they can be very useful in providing dry walking in low areas of a garden which always lie very marshy in the winter.

Amateurs, like professionals, should certainly try to obtain gravel for topping paths which is unwashed because it contains a proportion of fine clay which helps the surface to bind together after it has been wetted and rolled.

As specified by Alison Hainey, to break the monotony of the gravel, in the area near the loggia where more of the ground was left unplanted, some quite widely spaced Heritage Old York paving slabs were used to form an abstract pattern of stepping-stones set in its surface. With the surface of the slabs level with that of the gravel, they provided a good visual transition between the more broken surface of the gravel and the smoother surface of the slabs used to form the loggia terrace.

Because large slabs were used for the terracing at Chelsea, as in private gardens, they could be laid on a thick bed of well-consolidated sharp sand over compacted soil. Had smaller slabs or cobbles been selected for terracing, to remain level when coping with heavy foot traffic, they would have needed a substantial compacted hard-core base layer below the sand.

The good binding qualities of unwashed gravel were exploited to make the treads of the flight of shallow, broad and deep steps used to help visitors negotiate the hill down from the loggia to the exit. Very stout timbers held on their edge by steel pickets driven deep into the ground were used to make the 'risers' and then the gravel was packed in behind them and consolidated with the vibrating roller. Steps like this are quick and easy to make and look much more appropriate to a woodland situation than more formal steps made of stone or brick.

Before planting, the last of the civil engineering work was inserting the large resin and glass-fibre pool liners into the cavities which had been previously dug for them. Although these liners are very tough and crack-resistant, water is heavy and it was important to be sure that all their exterior surfaces were fully supported. This was achieved by bedding them into a thick layer of sand and cramming sand and soil into the gap between the liner and the wall of the cavity until its level was flush with that of the liner rim. Although a 4 in (10 cm) layer of concrete reinforced with tough steel mesh could have been used to line the pools, given good support, resin and glass-fibre liners are more satisfactory because they are less prone to damage by frost. Furthermore, concrete should only be chosen if the shape and size of liner demanded by the design of the water feature cannot be matched by the resin liners available at specialist garden centres. In nature, most pools have dark bottoms, which makes them such wonderful mirrors to reflect the moods of the sky, so when it was in place at Chelsea the pool liner

was given a coat of matt black, water-resistant paint which would ultimately have become crusted with a layer of very dark green and brown algae.

Nothing seems more unnatural than a pond in which an artificial lining is evident. To mask the edges of the liner at Chelsea, Cliftons used the well-tried technique of using attractive rocks to overhang the edges in places and trailing plants to mask them in others. When the rocks had been settled in place and the hard structural work was completed the garden was ready for planting (see also Chapter 5 for information on selecting and planting your woodland plants).

A mature tree makes a fine backing for a circular rustic seat offering views in all directions. It is also the ideal place to hang a nesting box.

When selecting Alison Hainey's design as the winner of the Woodland Garden competition, the judges had great difficulty in discriminating between it and those submitted by the runners-up or the entrants whose designs were ultimately highly commended. On the pages which follow the designers are introduced and some of the best features of their designs are illustrated and discussed.

KEVAN
CHAMBERS

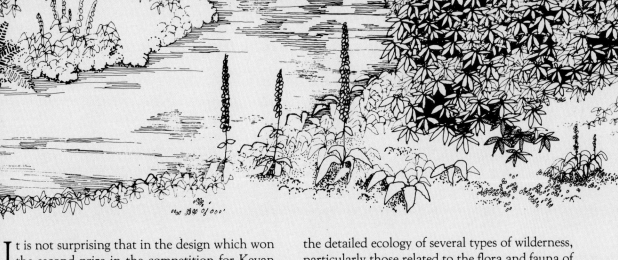

CHAPTER THREE

Exciting Alternatives

His research experience led wild flower expert Dr Kevan Chambers to submit
a design in which water and aquatic plants were prominently featured.

It is not surprising that in the design which won
the second prize in the competition for Kevan
Chambers of Manchester, water featured so
prominently, because for three years in carrying
out the research into sedimentology which gained
him his doctorate at Reading University he spent
most of his time working on and around
Brotherswater in the Lake District. While trying to
understand the source in the surrounding hills and
the ultimate fate of the materials sedimenting on
the lake bottom, he became intimately aware of
the detailed ecology of several types of wilderness,
particularly those related to the flora and fauna of
an aquatic and marshy lake shore. This increased
his understanding and love of wilder landscapes
which had been aroused by the previous three
years spent studying geography at Cambridge. It
also made him realise that he would like to apply
his knowledge by bringing some of the joy he ex-
perienced in wild places to people living in
crowded towns. To be able to do this with
authority he knew that he would need a

PLANTING PLAN

SPECIMEN TREES

A – *Acer campestre*
B – *Sorbus aria* 'Lutescens'
C – *Tilia cordata*
D – *Tilia platyphyllos*
E – *Prunus avium*
F – *Prunus padus*
G – *Malus sylvestris*
H – *Sorbus aucuparia*

SPECIMEN SHRUBS

1. – *Viburnum lantana*
2. – *Cytisus scoparius*
3. – *Viburnum opulus*
4. – *Acer palmatum* 'Atropurpureum'
5. – *Corylus avellana*
6. – *Pieris formosa forrestii*
7. – *Acer palmatum*
8. – *Camellia japonica* 'Adolphe Audusson'
9. – *Euonymus europaeus*
10. – *Mahonia aquifolium*
11. – *Acer palmatum* 'Dissectum'
12. – *Azalea mollis* 'Mrs L. J. Endtz' (Yellow)
13. – *Azalea* 'Coccinea Speciosa' (Orange red)
14. – *Rhododendron praecox* (Pink/Mauve)
15. – *Rhodo.* 'Polar Bear' (White)
16. – *Rhodo.* 'Purple Splendour' (Dark Purple)
17. – *Rhodo.* 'Earl of Donoughmore' (Red)
18. – *Rhodo.* 'Lavender Girl' (Lavender)
19. – *Rhodo.* 'Albrechtii' (Pink)
20. – *Rhodo. luteum* (Yellow)
21. – *Rhodo.* 'Sapphire' (Blue)
22. *Cyclamen hederifolium* (Wild Cyclamen)
Oxalis acetosella (Wood Sorrel)
Primula vulgaris (Primrose)
Viola odorata (Sweet Violet)
23. *Juncus effusus* (Rush)
Caltha palustris (Marsh Marigold)
Ajuga reptans (Bugle)
Lychnis flos-cuculi (Ragged Robin)
Asplenium scolopendrium (Hart's-tongue Fern)
Leucojum aestivum (Loddon Lily)
24. *Galanthus nivalis* (Snowdrop)
Primula vulgaris (Primrose)
Convallaria majalis (Lily of the Valley)
25. *Athyrium filix-femina* (Lady Fern)
Digitalis purpurea (Foxglove)

Campanula trachelium (Nettle-leaved Bellflower)
Mercurialis perennis (Dog's Mercury)
26. *Cyclamen hederifolium* (Wild Cyclamen)
Silene dioica (Red Campion)
Asplenium scolopendrium (Hart's-tongue Fern)
Gymnocarpium dryopteris (Oak Fern)
Primula vulgaris (Primrose)
27. *Primula vulgaris* (Primrose)
Galium odoratum (Sweet Woodruff)
Gymnocarpium dryopteris (Oak Fern)
Leucojum vernum (Spring Snowflake)
28. *Stellaria holostea* (Greater Stitchwort)
Silene dioica (Red Campion)
Ranunculus ficaria (Lesser Celandine)
Dryopteris pseudomas (Golden Male Fern)
Narcissus pseudonarcissus (Wild Daffodil)
29. *Silene dioica* (Red Campion)
Campanula rotundifolia (Harebell)

Cirsium heterophyllum (Melancholy Thistle)
Saxifraga granulata (Meadow Saxifrage)
Narcissus pseudonarcissus (Wild Daffodil)
30. *Polygonatum multiflorum* (Solomon's Seal)
Primula elatior (Oxlip)
Solidago virgaurea (Golden Rod)
Teucrium scorodonia (Wood Sage)
31. *Primula veris* (Cowslip)
Geranium pratense (Meadow Cranesbill)
Stachys officinalis (Betony)
Sanguisorba officinalis (Great Burnet)
Scabiosa columbaria (Small Scabious)
Filipendula vulgaris (Dropwort)
Centaurea nigra (Hard Heads)
Centaurea scabiosa (Greater Knapweed)
Narcissus pseudonarcissus (Wild Daffodil)
Chrysanthemum leucanthemum (Ox-eye Daisy)
32. *Rosa canina* (Dog Rose)
Seeding:
Open areas.

qualification in landscape architecture which he acquired after a two-year period at Newcastle University. There he learnt the skills necessary to integrate the ingredients of a natural landscape on the smaller stretches of land usually available for development in the industrial areas of cities dedicated to urban renewal. Sadly, however, like most prophets, he was somewhat ahead of his time and when, in the autumn of 1981, *The Sunday Times* Wildlife Garden Competition was announced, he had spent two years in trying to interest municipal authorities in his projects without much success. Fortunately, during that period he occupied himself with his hobby of collecting and propagating British native wild plants and was building up a considerable stock of

A simple kissing gate allowing pedestrian access and a farm gate for cars flanked by picket fencing makes a very effective and appropriate entrance and boundary to a woodland garden.

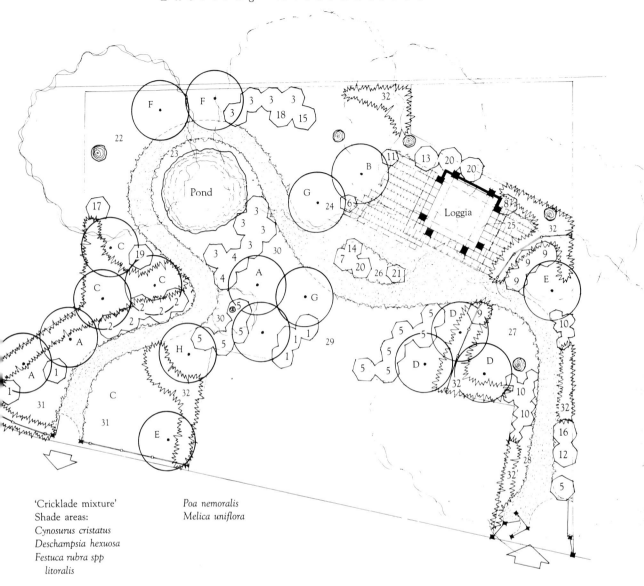

'Cricklade mixture'
Shade areas:
Cynosurus cristatus
Deschampsia hexuosa
Festuca rubra spp
   litoralis

Poa nemoralis
Melica uniflora

them. With an outstanding design he won that competition and subsequent to that success he has been able to establish NPK Landlife Ltd, which offers a conservation design service which has begun to flourish. One of its greatest strengths is that it also operates a nursery business selling British native plants derived from the stock of mother plants which Kevan Chambers built up during his period of unemployment

Apart from a most attractive design it was Kevan Chambers' subtle way of using wildflowers to maximum effect which most impressed the judges in the Woodland Garden competition and convinced them that he should win another prize. While appreciating why he had devoted so much plot space to a large pond situated right in the heart of the garden, they felt that after the deep excavation which would be entailed in forming its southern bank, a good deal of costly walling would be necessary to hold back the remaining earth, particularly as the track of the main pathway was to remain directly above it. However, they were particularly charmed by the way in which Kevan Chambers had, by clever planting of trees and shrubs, compartmentalised the garden so that a variety of different environments offering different pleasures would be perceived in succession without more than one of them being seen easily from any one point in a journey through the garden. The features which the judges greatly appreciated on a notional walk from the entrance to the exit are described overleaf.

The simple farm and kissing gates they felt had an attractive woodland feel.

The mostly yellow and red flowering plants like lesser celandines, wild daffodils and red campions had been used in the first area to offer what would be a very bright welcome to the woodland in the spring.

The inclusion of the 'relics' of a post and rail fence as a support for honeysuckles and dog roses to make the first division of the garden was considered a very thoughtful idea because it was the sort of feature often encountered and enjoyed on woodland walks.

In the first wide glade, which would tend to be seen most frequently in the summer when the loggia would be likely to be used often, the emphasis was placed on summer colour with the light blue of plants like harebells dominating the flower meadow and erect melancholy thistles offering strong structural interest. However, even in spring the area would be beautiful with an island shrubbery set in a widened area of the gravel path offering primroses, pink *Rhododendron praecox* and yellow *Rhododendron luteum*. The highly dissected foliage of *Acer palmatum* would prevent the island from ever looking dull and a carpet of *Cyclamen hederifolium* would guarantee autumn excitement.

In the pond, glade plants like marsh marigolds in the spring and pink ragged robin in the summer should, with the help of the aquatic plants, keep the area bright for many months.

The very beautiful low-growing oak and beech ferns with finely textured foliage which are often found creeping on the most attractive woodland floors would have given a great feeling of authenticity to the more heavily planted area beyond the pond, constrasting well with the soft neutral greens of the background.

The exit glade was clearly designed to become a butterfly paradise in summer with its brilliant white ox-eye daisies and small light blue scabious, likely both to attract and mimic their presence.

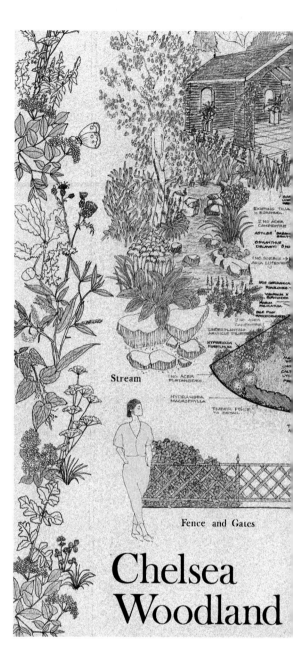

Stream

Fence and Gates

Chelsea Woodland

SUE ILLMAN AND YVONNE YOUNG

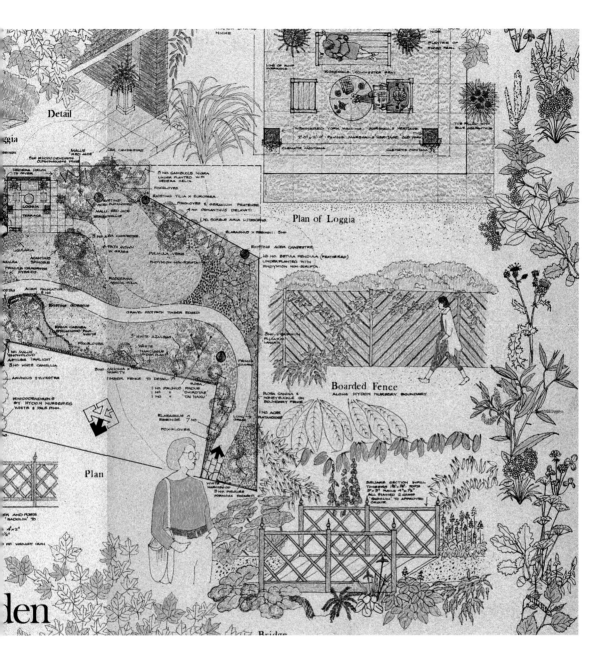

It was not long after Sue Illman and Yvonne Young of Cheltenham had formed a landscape practice that the Woodland Garden competition was announced and they decided that a successful entry might help it to become better known. Since doing well seemed particularly important to them they both admit that they spent many sleepless nights agonising over how to obtain the right balance between creating a natural woodland landscape and offering the additional interest for dedicated gardeners which the competition brief demanded. Their scrupulous attention to this sort of detail was well rewarded when their design won the third prize and high praise from the judges for both its lovely presentation and the sensitivity with which the plants had been deployed.

Their submission was considered notable because it contained a gurgling stream as well as a still pond, showing water in both its dynamic and placid moods. Contrived to appear to emerge from

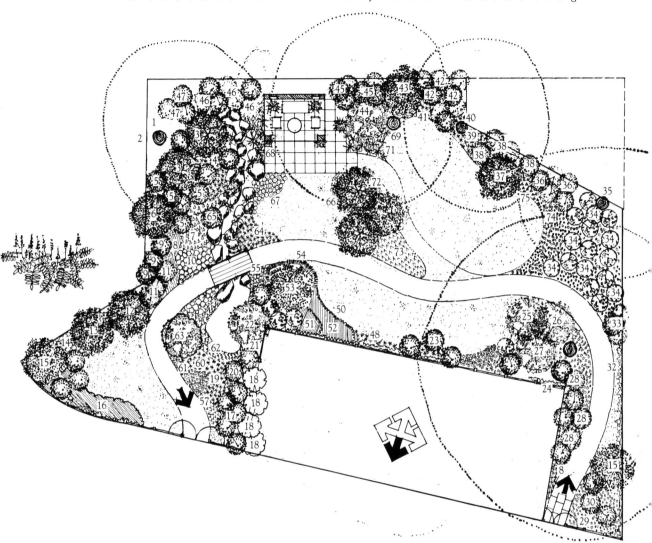

a spring hidden under deep canopy on the high land in the south-eastern corner of the garden, the stream was designed to capitalise on the asset of the steep slope towards the north where it could scamper down a series of rocky falls and shoot under a simple bridge made of stout planking before entering the calm of a low pond. The sound of water in its animated phase would provide a soothing background for people making desultory conversation as they relaxed in the loggia and enjoyed the view down to the pool, while its craggy edges would offer hundreds of exciting small niches to harbour marsh-loving plants.

With its open sides and front, the loggia was designed to allow extensive views and woodland sounds to be enjoyed by all its occupants. Although amply scaled, it was not felt that its presence in the woodland would be inappropriate

because its design was pleasingly simple. Sharing some of the bold solidity of a woodman's dry log store, its only real sophistications were a pair of mirror-backed niches set in its solid backing wall to reflect a pair of sword ferns set in the top of attractive, old, square sectioned, earthenware chimney pots.

Another notable feature of this design was the way in which Sue Illman and Yvonne Young managed the planting. Mimicking nature, they massed plants of a particular species, but to please serious gardeners, they exaggerated some of nature's best effects by allowing the masses to extend into great drifts. These would in turn develop stronger and stronger colour before fading to allow the attention to be diverted to other drifts which were just coming into full flower. Near the entrance a great stretch of primroses could greet a

PLANTING PLAN

1. Shrubs and trees under planted with *Hedera helix*
2. Existing *Tilia × europaea*
3. 2 No. *Acer campestre*
4. *Astilbe* 'Bressingham Beauty'
5. 5 No. *Osmanthus delavayi*
6. 1 No. *Sorbus aria* 'Lutescens'
7. *Iris germanica*
8. Foxgloves
9. *Viburnum × burkwoodii*
10. *Rheum palmatum*
11. Pale pink Rhododendron
12. 2 No. *Acer campestre*
13. Underplanting *Aruncus sylvester*
14. *Hypericum hirstutum*
15. 1 No. *Acer platanoides*
16. *Hydrangea macrophylla*
17. 4 No. pale pink Azaleas
18. Rhododendrons by Hydon Nurseries white & pale pink
19. *Aruncus sylvester*
20. 3 No. White Camellia

21. *Astilbe* 'Irrlicht'
22. 1 No. *Malus* 'Snowcloud'
23. 3 No. *Mahonia* 'Charity'
24. *Rosa*
25. 1 No. *Prunus padus*
26. 1 No. *Prunus* 'Shirotae'
27. 1 No. *Prunus* 'Tai Haku'
28. *Elaeagnus × ebbingii* 7 No.
29. White Narcissus
30. 3 No. *Pieris formosa forrestii*
31. 1 No. *Acer platanoides*
32. *Rosa canina* & Honeysuckle on boundary fence
33. 3 No. *Viburnum plicatum* 'Lanarth'
34. 16 No. *Betula pendula* (feathered) under-planted with *Endymion non-scripta*
35. Existing *Acer campestre*
36. 5 No. *Elaeagnus × ebbingii*
37. 1 No. *Sorbus aria* 'Lutescens'
38. 4 No. *Osmanthus delavayi*
39. Foxgloves & *Geranium pratense*
40. Existing *Tilia × europaea*

41. Foxgloves
42. 5 No. *Sambucus nigra* underplanted with *Hedera helix*
43. *Acer campestre*
44. *Malus* 'Red Jade'
45. 5 No. *Rhododendron* 'Cunningham's White'
46. 7 No. *Elaeagnus × ebbingii*
47. 3 No. *Viburnum tinus*
48. Foxgloves
49. Foxgloves
50. *Erica carnea*
51. *Erica carnea* 'Springwood pink'
52. *Erica carnea* 'Springwood white'
53. Existing *Quercus*
54. 3 No. *Acer palmatum*
55. Hostas
56. 1 No. *Malus* 'Snowcloud'
57. *Astilbe* 'Irrlicht'
58. 3 No. White Camelia
59. *Aruncus sylvester*
60. *Lychnis flos-cuculi* Ferns
61. *Caltha palustris*
62. Hostas
63. *Malus* 'Red Sentinel'
64. *Primula × chungensis* hybrids
65. Azalea
66. *Acanthus spinosus*
67. Ligularia
68. Ferns

69. Existing *Acer platanoides*
70. *Malus* 'Red Jade'
71. Hemerocallis
72. 3 No. *Acer campestre*
73. *Rodgersia aesculifolia*
74. *Endymion non-scripta*
75. *Primula veris*

visitor in spring before their attention was drawn to a solid carpet of bluebells clothing the soft floor beneath the trees and shrubs beyond.

Breaking into the first large glade in the spring, swatches of foxgloves, pink and white ericas and white narcissi would dominate, while ceding that role in' summer to a vast promontory of tall bronze-leaved white-flowered *Rodgersia aesculifolia*. Featuring largely in the smaller glade outside the loggia terrace, hybrid primulas in spring would be followed by showy orange-yellow flowered *Ligularia dentata* later in the year. The same bold treatment was adopted for the planting around the pool with a forest of rhubarb-leaved large rheums backing a solid prairie of hostas and a creamy foam of feathery *Aruncus sylvester*.

In many respects these designers used their herbaceous plants in a way reminiscent of that employed by the great Brazilian landscaper and abstract painter Roberto Burle Marx who has described his technique as painting with flowers. Critics of the technique have suggested that it is too painterly and therefore two-dimensional, but Sue Illman and Yvonne Young in their design for Chelsea could never be accused of that because they placed their taller shrubs and semi-mature trees in such a way as to exploit their verticality and subtly vary the contours and forms en-countered when viewing the garden from any one place. A good example would be the way in which they placed the malus trees to dominate the hostas in the pool area. As sentinels standing guard on either side of the pool, red and white flowered crab apples, while seeming aloof, would contrast beautifully and beckon for the attention of people in the loggia on bright days in May.

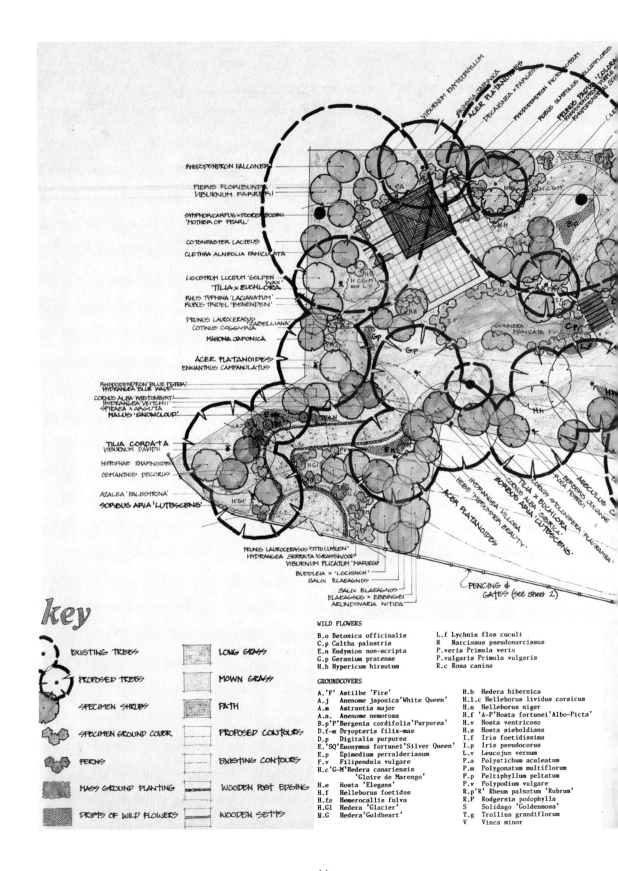

RHODODENDRON FALCONERI

PIERIS FLORIBUNDA
VIBURNUM FARRERI

SYMPHORICARPUS × DOORENBOSII
'MOTHER OF PEARL'

COTONEASTER LACTEUS
CLETHRA ALNIFOLIA PANICULATA

LIGUSTRUM LUCIDUM 'GOLDEN WAX'
TILIA × EUCHLORA
RHUS TYPHINA 'LACIANATUM'
RUBUS TRIDEL 'BENENDEN'

PRUNUS LAUROCERASUS 'ZABELLIANA'
COTINUS COGGYRIA

MAHONIA JAPONICA

ACER PLATANOIDES
ENKIANTHUS CAMPANULATUS

RHODODENDRON 'BLUE PETER'
HYDRANGEA 'BLUE WAVE'
CORNUS ALBA 'WESTONBIRT'
HYDRANGEA 'VEITCHII'
SPIRAEA × ARGUTA
MALUS 'SNOWCLOUD'

TILIA CORDATA
VIBURNUM DAVIDII

HIPPOPHAE RHAMNOIDES
OSMANTHUS DECORUS

AZALEA 'PALESTRINA'
SORBUS ARIA 'LUTESCENS'

PRUNUS LAUROCERASUS 'OTTO LUYKEN'
HYDRANGEA SERRATA 'GRAYSWOOD'
VIBURNUM PLICATUM 'MARIESII'
BUDDLEIA × 'LOCHINCH'
SALIX ELAEAGNOS
SALIX ELAEAGNOS
ELAEAGNUS × EBBINGEI
ARUNDINARIA NITIDA

VIBURNUM RHYTIDOPHYLLUM
PHORMIUM TENAX
ACER PLATANOIDES
PECANSNEA × FARGESII
RHODODENDRON PONTICUM
RUBUS OLMIFOLIUS 'ELLIPFLORUS'
PRUNUS PADUS 'COLORATA'
RHODODENDRON PONTICUM
RHODODENDRON SCHI

PENCING &
GATES (see sheet 2)

key

EXISTING TREES

PROPOSED TREES

SPECIMEN SHRUBS

SPECIMEN GROUND COVER

FERNS

MASS GROUND PLANTING

DRIFTS OF WILD FLOWERS

LONG GRASS

MOWN GRASS

PATH

PROPOSED CONTOURS

EXISTING CONTOURS

WOODEN POST EDGING

WOODEN SETTS

WILD FLOWERS

B.o Betonica officinalis
C.p Caltha palustris
E.n Endymion non-scripta
G.p Geranium pratense
H.h Hypericum hirsutum

L.f Lychnis flos cuculi
N   Narcissus pseudonarcissus
P.veris Primula veris
P.vulgaris Primula vulgaris
R.c Rosa canina

GROUNDCOVERS

A.'F' Astilbe 'Fire'
A.j   Anenome japonica 'White Queen'
A.m   Astrantia major
A.n.   Anenome nemorosa
B.p'P' Bergenia cordifolia 'Purpurea'
D.f-m Dryopteris filix-mas
D.p   Digitalis purpurea
E.'SQ' Euonymus fortunei 'Silver Queen'
E.p   Epimedium perralderianum
F.v   Filipendula vulgare
H.c'G-M' Hedera canariensis
           'Gloire de Marengo'
H.e   Hosta 'Elegans'
H.f   Helleborus foetidus
H.f²   Hemerocallis fulva
H.Gl   Hedera 'Glacier'
H.G   Hedera 'Goldheart'

H.h   Hedera hibernica
H.l.c Helleborus lividus corsicus
H.n   Helleborus niger
H.f 'A-P'Hosta fortunei 'Albo-Picta'
H.v   Hosta ventricosa
H.s   Hosta sieboldiana
I.f   Iris foetidissima
I.p   Iris pseudocorus
L.v   Leucojum vernum
P.a   Polystichum aculeatum
P.m   Polygonatum multiflorum
P.p   Peltiphyllum peltatum
P.v   Polypodium vulgare
R.p'R' Rheum palmatum 'Rubrum'
R.P   Rodgersia podophylla
S   Solidago 'Goldenmosa'
T.g   Trollius grandiflorum
V   Vinca minor

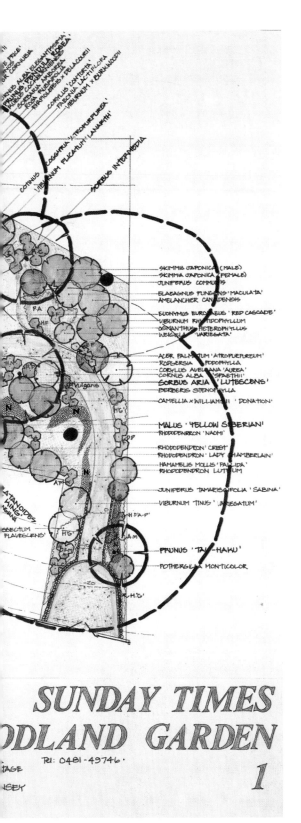

SKIMMIA JAPONICA (MALE)
SKIMMIA JAPONICA (FEMALE)
JUNIPERUS COMMUNIS

ELAEAGNUS PUNGENS 'MACULATA'
AMELANCHIER CANADENSIS

EUONYMUS EUROPAEUS 'RED CASCADE'
VIBURNUM RHYTIDOPHYLLUM
OSMANTHUS HETEROPHYLLUS
WEIGELA 'VARIEGATA'

ACER PALMATUM 'ATROPURPUREUM'
RODGERSIA PODOPHYLLA
CORYLUS AVELLANA 'AUREA'
CORNUS ALBA 'SPAETHII'
SORBUS ARIA 'LUTESCENS'
BERBERIS STENOPHYLLA

CAMELLIA x WILLIAMSII 'DONATION'

MALUS 'YELLOW SIBERIAN'
RHODODENDRON 'NAOMI'

RHODODENDRON 'CREST'
RHODODENDRON 'LADY CHAMBERLAIN'
HAMAMELIS MOLLIS 'PALLIDA'
RHODODENDRON LUTEUM

JUNIPERUS TAMARISCIFOLIA 'SABINA'

VIBURNUM 'TINUS' 'VARIEGATUM'

PRUNUS 'TAI-HAKU'

FOTHERGILLA MONTICOLOR

SUNDAY TIMES
ODLAND GARDEN
TEL: 0481-49746
1

AMANDA
BLICQ

One of the great strengths in Amanda Blicq's submission for the competition was undoubtedly the great subtlety of its planting – but this is to be expected from someone who obtained a degree in environmental science from London University before going on to do a post-graduate course in landscape architecture at Sheffield. To her academic qualifications she added five years practical landscaping experience in both private practice and public authority work in Yorkshire, Nottinghamshire and Sydney, Australia, before setting up her own practice in Guernsey.

The layout of Amanda Blicq's garden is designed to provide a variety of spatial experiences when moving along a path which meanders around the site constantly changing direction. Introducing so many curves made its track much longer than any rational direct route from the entrance to the exit and this would offer more time for the visitor to enjoy the garden and appreciate its many nuances. It also makes the site seem much larger than it is. To make the path readily acceptable to people in wheelchairs, some excavation was envisaged to reduce the gradients near both the entrance and the exit and a log palisade was considered the safest and most appropriate way of preventing the soil from collapsing into these cuttings. As far as possible, the main path avoids contact with the site boundary, the fencing being screened behind planting and in shadow wherever that is feasible, and it actually passes through the loggia area. This was one of the rare designs in which that option was adopted. In order to break the tedium of the gravel in places, notably near the entrance and exit where the paths widened, log stepping-stones were sunk into its surface. In order to blur the margins of the rectangular Hydon site, many further

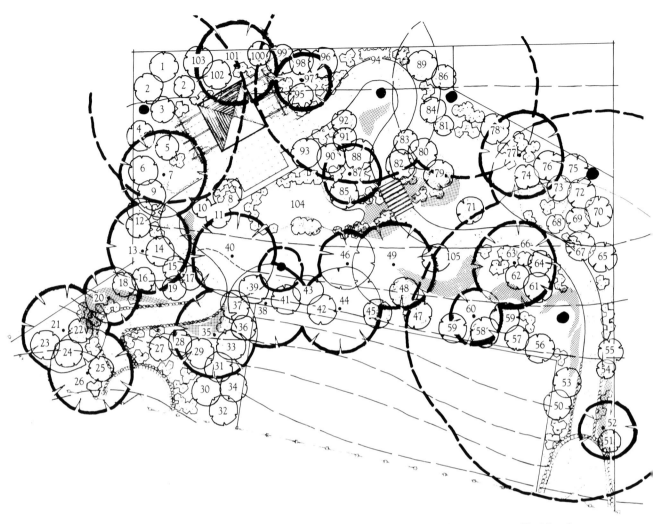

PLANTING PLAN

1. *Rhododendron* 'Falconer'
2. *Pieris floribunda Viburnum farreri*
3. *Symphoricarpos × doorenbosii* 'Mother of Pearl'
4. *Cotoneaster lacteus*
5. *Clethra alnifolia paniculata*
6. *Ligustrum lucidum* 'Golden Wax'
7. *Tilia × euchlora*
8. *Rhus typhina* 'Lacianatum'
9. *Rubus × tridel* 'Benenden'
10. *Prunus laurocerasus* 'Zabelliana'
11. *Cotinus coggyria*
12. *Mahonia japonica*
13. *Acer platanoides*
14. *Enkianthus campanulatus*
15. *Rhododendron* 'Blue Peter'
16. *Hydrangea* 'Blue Wave'
17. *Cornus alba* 'Westonbirt'
18. *Hydrangea* 'Veitchii'
19. *Spiraea × arguta*
20. *Malus* 'Snowcloud'
21. *Tilia cordata*
22. *Viburnum davidii*
23. *Hippophae rhamnoides*
24. *Osmanthus decorus*
25. *Azalea* 'Palestrina'
26. *Sorbus aria* 'Lutescens'
27. *Prunus laurocerasus* 'Otto Luyken'
28. *Hydrangea serrata* 'Grayswood'
29. *Viburnum plicatum* 'Mariesii'
30. *Buddleia × fallowiana* 'Lochinch'
31. *Salix elaeagnos*
32. *Salix elaeagnos*
33. *Elaeagnus × ebbingei*
34. *Arundinaria nitida*
35. *Acer platanoides*
36. *Hebe* 'Midsummer Beauty'
37. *Hydrangea villosa*
38. *Sorbus aria* 'Lutescens'
39. *Cornus alba* 'Sibirica'
40. *Tilia × euchlora*
41. *Cornus stolonifera* 'Flaviramea'
42. *Rosa moyesii*
43. *Berberis julianae*
44. *Aesculus carnea* 'Briotti'
45. *Eucryphia × intermedia*
46. *Prunus virginiana* 'Schubert'
47. *Prunus lusitanica*
48. *Magnolia × soulangiana*
49. *Acer platanoides* 'Crimson King'
50. *Acer palmatum* 'Dissectum Flavescens'
51. *Fothergilla monticolor*
52. *Prunus* 'Tai-Haku'
53. *Viburnum tinus* 'Variegatum'
54. *Juniperus sabina tamariscifolia*
55. *Rhododendron luteum*
56. *Hamamelis mollis* 'Pallida'
57. *Rhododendron* 'Lady Chamberlain'
58. *Rhododendron* 'Crest'
59. *Rhododendron* 'Naomi'
60. *Malus* 'Yellow Siberian'
61. *Camellia × williamsii* 'Donation'

Woodland gardens can be enchanting places and it pays to make some sort of loggia so that they can be enjoyed even in the rain. And it is in the surrounds of a loggia where keen gardeners can indulge their pleasure in ornamental planting without disturbing the natural appearance elsewhere.

62. Berberis × stenophylla
63. Sorbus aria 'Lutescens'
64. Cornus alba 'Spaethii'
65. Corylus avellana 'Aurea'
66. Rodgersia podophylla
67. Acer palmatum 'Atropurpureum'
68. Weigela 'Variegata'
69. Osmanthus heterophyllus
70. Viburnum rhytidophyllum
71. Euonymus europaeus 'Red Cascade'
72. Amelanchier canadensis
73. Elaeagnus pungens 'Maculata'
74. Juniperus communis
75. Skimmia japonica (female)
76. Skimmia japonica (male)
77. Sorbus intermedia

78. Viburnum plicatum 'Lanarth'
79. Cotinus coggyria 'Atropurpurea'
80. Viburnum × burkwoodii
81. Paeonia lactiflora
82. Corylus avellana 'Contorta'
83. Rhaphiolepis × delacourii
84. Rosa rubrifolia
85. Sorbaria arborea
86. Rubus cockburniensis
87. Prunus 'Pendula Rosea'
88. Cornus alba 'Elegantissima'
89. Cotoneaster 'Cornubia'
90. Salix elaeagnos
91. Viburnum tinus 'Eve Price'
92. Pieris formosa forrestii
93. Fatsia japonica

94. Clematis vitalba
95. Rhododendron schlippenbachii
96. Rhododendron 'Purple Splendour'
97. Prunus padus 'Colorata'
98. Rubus ulmifolius 'Bellidiflorus'
99. Rhododendron fictolacteum
100. Decaisnea Fargesii
101. Acer platanoides
102. Skimmia japonica
103. Viburnum rhytidophyllum
104. Gunnera manicata
105. Kolkwitsia amabilis

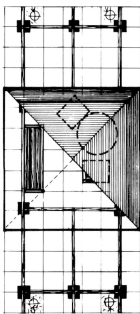

rhododendrons were less formally planted along its edges.

Four tall Heritage Old York stone plinths were used as the bases for stout rectangular timber pillars to support the pitched roof of the square, open-sided, loggia. Two further lines of three pillars set on the east and west side of the loggia were designed to support timber pergolas.

Despite the difficulty of the site, Amanda Blicq decided it was essential to locate the pond just below the loggia terrace so that visitors leaning or sitting on a wall which she provided for the purpose at the terrace edge could peer into its depths. Because of its situation she could extend a marshy area for a considerable distance beyond the western end of the pond, finally allowing it to peter out deep in the canopy of a shrubbery. This meant that both sun and intense shade-loving bog plants could be present in the garden. It also suggested the introduction of a delightful feature – a board walk – as part of the main path where it crosses the marshy land. This would allow visitors to examine such marsh plants as *Caltha palustris*, *Iris foetidissima* or ferns at close quarters.

The main glade in Amanda Blicq's garden was to be located in front of the loggia because the heaviest planting was confined to the garden margins. This ensured that all the surface of the pond would be exposed to bright light for most of the day and the reflective nature would be as obvious as possible and therefore able to impress its character on the surrounding area, offering a diversity of visual experiences to people pausing at the loggia.

The restraint in the planting nominated for this garden is particularly praise-worthy. Any unruly, over-concentration and massing of bright colours which might resemble a public park planting and look quite out of place in a woodland

Amanda Blicq opted to use an attractive variant on simplex board fencing. By setting the boards obliquely on their frame she made them echo the way in which branches grow from tree trunks.

has been avoided. This means that visitors would be able to enjoy the character of the foliage and the overall plant forms, which are often overlooked, without distraction.

In each separate area of the garden, one, or at the most two, harmonious colours provided by either flower, stem or foliage have been chosen to dominate, and on the whole the discreeter, more pastel, shades have been selected.

Stronger coloured plants have been used to direct viewers to focal points, eg from the loggia across the pond to the *Acer platanoides* 'Crimson King' or from the entrance gate to the golden hazel and *Acer palmatum* 'Atropurpureum' a long way ahead.

The planting itself is designed to give year-round interest to the viewer with autumn and winter flowering shrubs, and use of plants with stem effects (*Cornus* 'Sibirica' and 'Flaviramea'), berries or decorative foliage effects. Each section of the garden has a colour theme, beginning at the entrance with a yellow theme of *Hedera* 'Goldheart', *Acer* 'Dissectum Flavescens', *Rhododendron luteum* and golden hazel, emphasised by daffodils and primroses in spring and golden rod in autumn.

The central section has a theme of pink and purple foliage and flowers, beginning with *Magnolia soulangiana*, and *Kolkwitzia amabilis* and *Viburnum plicatum* later in the year. *Cotinus coggygria* 'Atropurpurea' and *Rosa rubrifolia* continue the theme. *Iris foetidissima* beneath a hedgerow of dog roses add a further element of purple, and the *Acer platanoides* 'Crimson King' and *Aesculus carnea* 'Briotti' are the focal point of the larger meadow area, and through glimpsed views, of the entire site.

Beyond the loggia, the theme is blue and white, emphasised by bluebells and meadow cranesbill, and continued in the use of *Vinca minor*, hydrangea and silver grey foliage plants such as *Hippophae rhamnoides* and *Elaeagnus × ebbingei* and *Hedera* 'Glacier'. In using stout planks set diagonally and alternating their direction in adjacent panels, Amanda Blicq tried to produce a surround fencing and gates which were appropriate to a woodland, while at the same time original in character. At the junction of pairs of panels she raised the level of the diagonal timbers, developing them into a leaf motif.

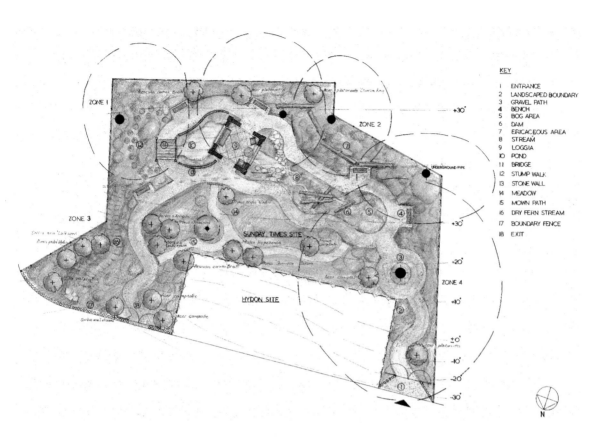

KEY

1	ENTRANCE
2	LANDSCAPED BOUNDARY
3	GRAVEL PATH
4	BENCH
5	BOG AREA
6	DAM
7	ERICACEOUS AREA
8	STREAM
9	LOGGIA
10	POND
11	BRIDGE
12	STUMP WALK
13	STONE WALL
14	MEADOW
15	MOWN PATH
16	DRY FERN STREAM
17	BOUNDARY FENCE
18	EXIT

GILLIAN SARSON

A training in graphic design at Guildford School of Art led Gillian Sarson into several years of teaching before a growing family demanded her full-time presence at home in London. As a housewife and mother she obtained great pleasure from her garden and she used it as an outlet for her artistic talents while the children were growing up. In 1985–6, with her motherly duties becoming less onerous, she took a garden design course at the Pershore College of Agriculture with a view to beginning a second career. The announcement of the Woodland Garden competition seemed to

provide her with a wonderful opportunity to put some of her Pershore lessons into practice and in many respects her submission was one of the most notable among the entries received. Its particular strengths were in her handling of the hard architectural features of the garden. With its classical lines, large *oeil de boeuf* windows, balancing walk-through arched doorways in the other two walls and beautifully proportional lantern crowning the roof, her loggia would have looked perfectly at home gracing Stowe or Stourhead and it is a design to which one feels Repton or William Kent would not have been too proud to attach their names. To people inter-preting a woodland garden as something totally rustic and barely touched by man, this loggia would seem too intrusive and formal and perhaps overscaled in a garden of this size, but there are many ways of strangling a dinosaur and clearly Gillian Sarson took a more sophisticated view and opted for a garden with a more blatantly romantic flavour – and like all the great romantic designers she played many tricks. She wanted to give the im-pression that her loggia provided views over, and

PLANTING PLAN

TREES

2 No. *Aesculus carnea* 'Briotti'
3 No. *Acer campestre*
2 No. *Acer platanoides*
1 No. *Acer platanoides* 'Crimson King'
1 No. *Tilia cordata*
1 No. *Tilia platphyllus*
1 No. *Sorbus aria* 'Lutescens'
2 No. *Sorbus intermedia*
2 No. *Prunus padus* 'Wateri'
1 No. *Prunus × yedoensis*
1 No. *Prunus sargentii*
1 No. *Prunus* 'Shimidsu Sakura'
1 No. *Malus hupehensis*

ZONE ONE

1. *Hosta plantaginea grandiflora*
2. *Rheum palmatum* 'Atrosanguineum'
3. *Miscanthus sacchariflorus*
4. *Osmunda regalis*
5. *Peltiphyllum peltatum*
6. *Typha minima*
7. *Juncus effusus*
8. *Caltha palustris*
9. *Lychnis flos-cuculi*
10. *Mimulus cupreus*
11. *Daphne laureola*
12. *Daphne pontica*
13. *Digitalis purpurea*
14. *Viburnum × juddii*
15. *Oxalis acetosella*
16. *Luzula maxima* 'Marginata'
17. *Viburnum tinus variegatum*
18. *Mahonia nervosa*
19. *Phillyrea decora*
20. *Stranvaesia salicifolia*
21. *Photinia × fraseri* 'Robusta'
22. *Arundinaria nitida*
23. *Arundinaria murielae*
24. *Mahonia aquifolium*
25. *Ruscus aculeatus*
26. *Rhododendron ponticum*
27. *Epimedium grandiflorum*
28. *Epimedium perralderianum*
29. *Primula vulgaris* 'Sibthorpii'
30. *Pulmonaria saccharata*
31. *Adiantum pedatum*

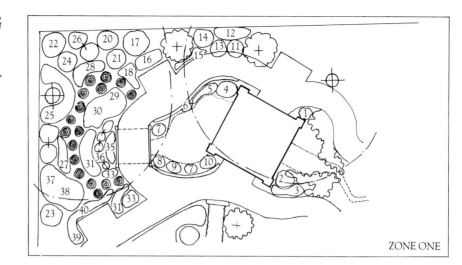

ZONE ONE

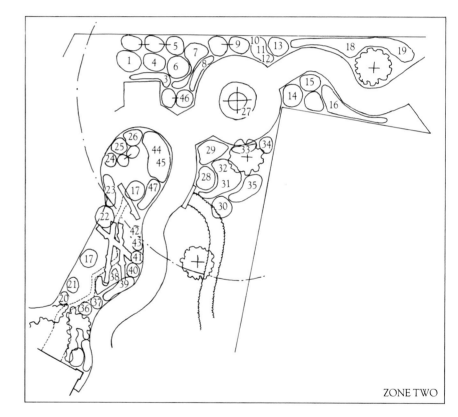

ZONE TWO

32. *Erythronium dens-canis*
33. *Hepatica transsilvanica*
34. *Viola labradorica*
35. *Sasa veitchii*
36. *Carex morrowii* 'Evergold'
37. *Endymion non-scripta*
38. *Allium ursinum*
39. *Bergenia purpurascens*
40. *Trillium grandiflorum*

ZONE TWO

1. *Cercidyphyllum japonicum*
2. *Osmanthus delavayi*
3. *Convallaria majalis*
4. *Polygonatum × hybridum*
5. *Mahonia fortunei*
6. *Hamamelis mollis*
7. *Lunaria rediviva*
8. *Blechnum penna-marina*
9. *Viburnum davidii*
10. *Hedera colchica*
11. *Narcissus spp*
12. *Helleborus foetidus*
13. *Lonicera pileata*
14. *Arundinaria nitida*
15. *Arundinaria viridistriata*
16. *Dryopteris erythrosora*

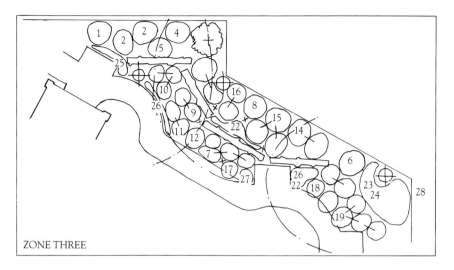

ZONE THREE

5. *Acer palmatum.* 'Dissectum'
6. *Acer palmatum* 'Senkaki'
7. *Acer palmatum* 'Dissectum Atropurpureum'
8. *Acer palmatum* 'Atropurpureum'
9. *Enkianthus campanulatus*
10. *Rhododendron loderi* 'King George'
11. *Rhododendron* 'Chink'
12. *Rhododendron keiskei*
13. *Rhododendron campylogynum*
14. *Rhododendron* 'Crest'
15. *Rhododendron macabeanum*
16. *Rhododendron hodgsonii*
17. *Azalea pontica*
18. *Pieris formosa forrestii*
19. *Skimmia japonica*
20. *Leucothoe fontanesiana*
21. *Leucothoe* 'Rubella'
22. *Smilacina racemosa*
23. *Cyclamen repandum*
24. *Galanthus nivalis*
25. *Vaccinium corymbosum*
26. *Hosta lancifolia*
27. *Hosta crispula*
28. *Lilium superbum*

17. *Osmunda regalis*
18. *Primula vulgaris*
19. *Ajuga reptans*
20. *Miscanthus sinensis variegatus*
21. *Eupatorium purpureum*
22. *Salix alba* 'Argentea'
23. *Hosta elata*
24. *Polypodium vulgare*
25. *Peltiphyllum peltatum*
26. *Mimulus guttatus*
27. *Hydrangea petiolaris*
28. *Hydrangea sargentiana*
29. *Endymion non scripta*

30. *Prunus laurocerasus*
31. *Trillium grandiflorum*
32. *Gymnocarpum dryopteris*
33. *Hepatica triloba*
34. *Viburnum tinus*
35. *Betonica officinalis*
36. *Lysichiton americanum*
37. *Carex pendula*
38. *Iris laevigata*
39. *Caltha palustris*
40. *Filipendula ulmaria*
41. *Scirpus albescens*
42. *Stachys palustris*
43. *Lychnis flos-cuculi*

44. *Primula denticulata*
45. *Primula japonica*
46. *Hypericum × indorum* 'Elstead'
47. *Astilbe × arendsii*

ZONE THREE

1. *Camellia × williamsii* 'J. C. Williams'
2. *Camellia japonica* 'Alba Simplex'
3. *Camellia* 'Gloire de Nantes'
4. *Magnolia × soulangiana*

This type of very elegant loggia which is expensive to build needs to harmonise with equally ambitious buildings and artefacts and be part of a woodland garden whose designer adopts a fully romantic attitude.

ZONE FOUR

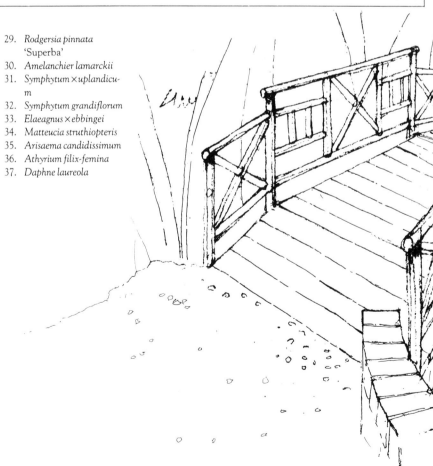

ZONE FOUR

1. *Rosa canina*
2. *Corylopsis pauciflora*
3. *Polygonatum hybridum*
4. *Elaeagnus commutata*
5. *Anemone nemorosa*
6. *Doronicum austriacum*
7. *Endymion non-scripta*
8. *Euphorbia robbiae*
9. *Crocus tomasinianus*
10. *Viola riviniana*
11. *Narcissus cyclamineus*
12. *Primula veris*
13. *Geranium pratense*
14. *Narcissus spp bulbocodium*
15. *Narcissus spp*
16. *Polypodium vulgare*
17. *Centaurea nigra*
18. *Vicia cracca*
19. *Eranthis hyemalis*
20. *Acer palmatum 'Senkaki'*
21. *Berberis × stenophylla*
22. *Bergenia purpurascens*
23. *Arundinaria falconeri*
24. *Polystichum setiferum divisilobum*
25. *Cotoneaster salicifolius*
26. *Blechnum penna-marina*
27. *Brunnera macrophylla*
28. *Rodgersia aesculifolia*
29. *Rodgersia pinnata 'Superba'*
30. *Amelanchier lamarckii*
31. *Symphytum × uplandicum*
32. *Symphytum grandiflorum*
33. *Elaeagnus × ebbingei*
34. *Matteucia struthiopteris*
35. *Arisaema candidissimum*
36. *Athyrium filix-femina*
37. *Daphne laureola*

was set on a bridge above, lots of water, so that visitors lingering there could look down over a clear mere on one side to see it disappear as a stream under a charming bridge which, although rustic, bore the stamp of a designer. While some surface water would be evident from the other window, much of the area would be marshy to simulate the emergence through the surface of water collected in an underground clay basin which, like a high dew pond in nature, could be the source of a small stream.

Despite using very simple wooden poles as the construction material in the design of this bridge (left) and gate (above) the eye of the sophisticated designer is obvious. They demonstrate one effective way of introducing novel and imaginative design notions into a woodland garden without disturbing its essentially sylvan mood.

For many of these effects Gillian Sarson was prepared to rely on illusion. By masking the outside edge of her bridge with thick shrubs so that the point of emergence of a stream from beneath it would be invisible, she could simply sit most of her bridge structure on a hump of dry land, allowing the water to lap against a hidden barrier just inside its loggia edge. She played a similar trick at the entrance and exit to the simulated tunnel below the loggia itself, which would also stand on solid ground. By these devices she considerably reduced the amount of excavation required to make her water feature and the cost of constructing both the loggia and the bridge – yes, those cost-conscious teachers of garden design at Pershore taught her well. Having learnt to lie with the building, she decided to baffle visitors further with her main path. She made it writhe and twist, spin round trees, divide and reunite, so that a visitor following its long track would quickly be confused by viewing the garden from a hundred different angles and ultimately stumble out of the exit convinced that it was very vast. To supplement the confusion and increase the excitement, she also created several other diverting pathways mown through meadow grass. Although they might seem excessive, she sited five seats in snug and leafy arbours from which the garden could be enjoyed. However, each of them would offer a quite different, but equally enchanting view. Gillian Sarson offered three features which were interesting and unique to the competition. The first was the creation of a large ericaceous area where the acid compost necessary would be held back as a shallow raised bed behind substantial logs laid out along the ground. In the far south-eastern corner of the garden, she adapted a nineteenth-century idea by making a walkway beneath the lime canopy marked out by attractive old moss-gathering tree stumps. Her third innovation was a dry stream cascading down the hill towards the exit formed by planting a thick 'stream' of ferns with the tallest towards the stream edges and the smallest suggesting the fast central current.

The whole garden was richly planted for effect. In a natural woodland there would be large areas occupied by a single species, but she sensibly felt that a woodland garden could be a pastiche of wild woodland with a great many more plants to interest keen gardeners.

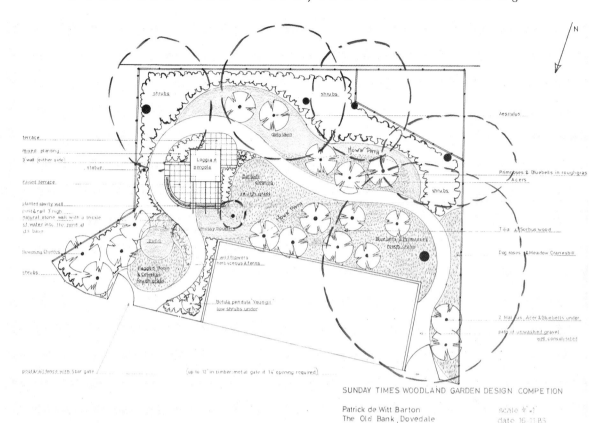

SUNDAY TIMES WOODLAND GARDEN DESIGN COMPETITION

Patrick de Witt Barton
The Old Bank, Dovedale

scale ⅛'=1'
date 16.11.85

PATRICK DE WITT BARTON

Like many of us, Patrick de Witt Barton had little interest in gardening until after he married, and doubtless his enthusiasm which had been fired by a visit to Hidcote would have remained that of the keen amateur if the firm for which he worked had not decided to move its head office away from his beloved Gloucestershire. Rather than be uprooted, he resigned and when equivalent work proved hard to find he restarted his career as a jobbing gardener.

When he was asked by a friend of one of his clients if he would like to 'make a bit of a garden round a pool', he said he would try, anticipating a job involving sticking a few plants around a small

pond. The pond, however, turned out to be a prestige swimming pool set in a largish plot of land which demanded a full landscape treatment. Undeterred, he did the job. The client was delighted and did not hesitate to recommend him to others requiring garden design work. Soon his reputation spread and these days he is so busy designing, that he hardly has time to touch a spade in his own, let alone anyone else's, garden.

Patrick Barton's approach to the woodland garden for Chelsea was to create a delicate counterpoint between a quite evidently gardened and tamed area in the vicinity of the loggia and a very natural woodland treatment elsewhere. He set the loggia more centrally in the garden than many other designers because he felt that it would then offer more vistas for people sitting in it and more views of it for people moving along the path passing it on three sides.

To increase the interest of the loggia area for gardeners, he attached an attractive wooden pergola to one side, supported at its outer margin on pillars in matching stone. In two places he terminated the terracing with low stone walls which made a good backing for small shrubberies beyond, and along approximately one-third of the

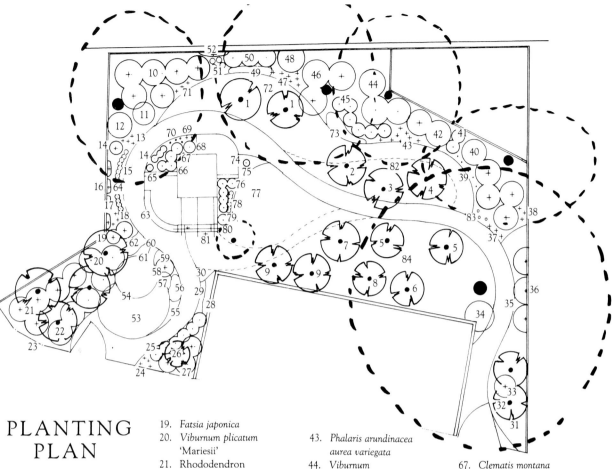

PLANTING PLAN

1. *Aesculus carnea* 'Briotti'
2. *Acer platanoides*
3. *Acer p.* 'Crimson King'
4. *Acer campestre*
5. *Sorbus aria* 'Lutescens'
6. *Sorbus intermedia*
7. *Tilia cordata*
8. *Tilia euchlora*
9. *Tilia platyphyllos*
10. Camellias
11. *Acer palmatum* 'Dissectum' under- planted with *Geranium pratense*
12. *Osmanthus delavayi*
13. *Polygonatum multiflorum Fatsia japonica*
14. *Pieris formosa forrestii*
15. *Euonymus* 'Emerald 'n Gold'
16. *Hedera canariensis* 'Gloire de Marengo'
17. This area planted with astilbes, euphorbias & foxgloves
18. *Polygonatum multiflorum*
19. *Fatsia japonica*
20. *Viburnum plicatum* 'Mariesii'
21. Rhododendron
22. *Osmanthus delavayi*
23. Flowering *Prunus* trees
24. *Bergenia cordifolia* & *Saxifraga umbrosa*
25. Evergreen Azaleas
26. *Betula pendula* 'Youngii'
27. *Mahonia aquifolium*
28. Meadow cranesbill
29. Betony
30. *Iris foetidissima*
31. Rough grass with bluebells
32. Flowering *Malus* trees
33. *Acer palmatum* 'Dissectum'
34. *Acer palmatum* 'Atropurpureum'
35. Rough grass with meadow cranesbill
36. *Rosa canina*
37. *Hosta* 'Honeybells'
38. White lilies
39. *Polystichum setiferum*
40. Rhododendrons
41. *Hypericum* 'Hidcote'
42. *Elaeagnus pungens* 'Maculata'
43. *Phalaris arundinacea aurea variegata*
44. *Viburnum rhytidophyllum*
45. Azaleas
46. *Enkianthus campanulatus*
47. Foxgloves
48. *Cotinus coggygria* 'Royal Purple'
49. *Alchemilla mollis*
50. *Cotoneaster* 'Cornubia'
51. *Verbascum × hybridum*
52. *Hedera helix* 'Gold Heart'
53. Rough grass, ragged robin, cowslips
54. Marsh marigold
55. Primulas
56. Euphorbia
57. Astilbe
58. *Acer palmatum*
59. Hostas
60. Ferns
61. *Hypericum hirsutum*
62. Astilbes
63. White petunias in wall
64. Statue
65. Fatshedera
66. 4 No. *Hydrangea* 'Whitewave'
67. *Clematis montana*
68. *Mahonia bealei*
69. *Iris pallida* var
70. *Aquilegia*
71. White lilies
72. Mown lawn with daisies
73. Bluebells and primroses
74. *Juniperus hibernica*
75. *Hedera helix* 'Glacier'
76. 5 No. Skimmia
77. Rough grass and daffodils
78. *Euonymus* 'Silver Queen'
79. *Hydrangea* 'White Wave'
80. *Clematis montana* 'Tetrarose'
81. *Cotoneaster horizontalis*
82. Rough grass with some bluebells, but mainly primroses
83. 3 No. *Euphorbia* 'Wupenii'
84. Rough grass with bluebells and a few primroses

terrace margin he specified a low curved stone wall topped by a planting trough to take annual plants like white petunias and an edging of trailers. To make it clear to visitors moving along the path that they were arriving at a special area, he stationed Britain's answer to the pencil cypress – a columnar Irish juniper on the western edge of the loggia planting.

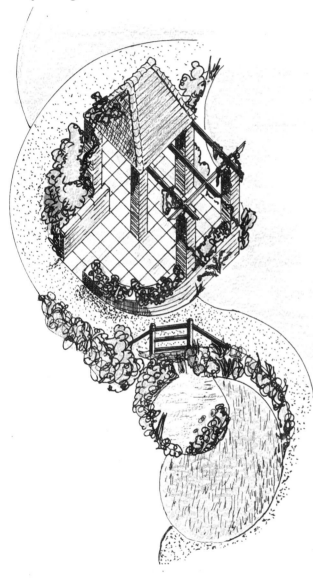

Within a few yards Patrick de Witt Barton has suggested two distinct environments. A pergola and planted walls round a loggia offer opportunities for intense gardening while nearby a portion of 3 barred fence provides a chance to simply lean and contemplate natural ponds and a wild flower meadow.

In the southern loggia shrubbery he allowed four *Hydrangea*, 'White Wave' and the tall *Mahonia bealei*, to dominate an underplanting of *Iris pallida* and aquilegia. Five *Skimmia japonica* above six *Euonymus* 'Silver Queen' with another *Hydrangea* 'White Wave' to contrast with the evergreen were used to fill the shrubbery on the other side of the loggia.

An ornamental hop and a *Clematis montana* 'Tetra Rose' were nominated to climb over the pergola – one stationed at the foot of each column which when mature would offer broken shade to contrast with the darker area below the loggia roof.

Looking west from the loggia, visitors would have a view over an open glade in the foreground where the rough grass would be studded with daffodils in the spring and self-seeded wildflowers, later to a copse of three species of *Acer*, lime and whitebeam trees with bluebells and primroses in the soft floor below.

The most notable feature to be seen to the south would be a large cluster of dark-leafed camellias acting as a suitable background for a bold planting of white lilies.

To the north, the main interest would lie in the pond area where on one flank a large *Acer palmatum* was envisaged overhanging a thick planting of astilbes, hostas, ferns and primulas, with many clusters of marsh marigold around the marshy pond edge.

Beyond the pond edge a large patch of rough grass would host a mass of cowslips intermingled with ragged robin – precisely what Patrick Barton observed when leaning on a fence overlooking a pond just down the road from his home in Gloucestershire in the early summer of 1986. When in November he started to design the garden at Chelsea, he remembered that fence and realised that in our gardens we provide too few places to merely lean and enjoy the view, so he included a length of fence in his design.

His attitude to the rest of the planting was to try as far as possible to maintain a good balance between evergreen and deciduous plants which would also spread their displays over as much of the season as possible and not seem to be too ornamental to be growing in a natural woodland surrounding.

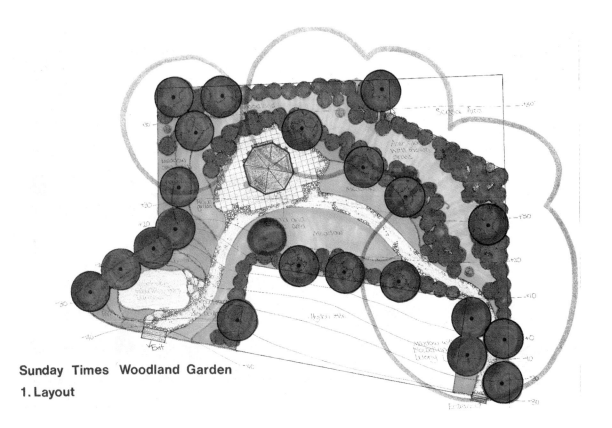

Sunday Times Woodland Garden

1. Layout

IRENE SHAW

A solid grounding in horticulture while studying for a degree at Wye College, London University, was for Irene Shaw a wonderful preparation for a career as a landscaper, which she began after obtaining a post-graduate diploma in landscape architecture at Manchester University. For the past twelve years she has exercised the talents which she developed as a designer on behalf of the Newcastle-upon-Tyne City Council where most of her work involves landscaping large-scale housing developments. She welcomed the Woodland Garden competition because it offered the

challenge of something quite different, and she determined that while her scheme would comply with the competition brief by including some genuine garden features, its overall flavour would be that of some of the lovely natural woodland in the more sheltered areas of the beautiful north and south Tyne valleys which she so enjoys with her family during her free time.

To this end she allowed the main path to follow the shortest route around the garden, simply making it swing around the obtruding Hydon site. This in nature might represent a country lane skirting a wood, with the fairly centrally located loggia set at its edge, substituting for what could be a woodman's cottage. This arrangement would mean that from everywhere along the main path there would be the possibility of contriving quite long vistas into the rest of the garden. It also allowed her to suggest the creation of a tall tree and shrub hedge running roughly parallel to the main path on its south side which swings behind the loggia. Given a very heavy planting along the east, west and southern margins of the plot, this hedge would conceal a wonderful secret area of the garden and to lure adventurous visitors along its leafy avenue she provided a simple path mown into the otherwise rough grass. Realising that there might be problems in creating a satisfactory high pool at Chelsea, Irene Shaw allowed her professional judgement to dictate that it should be located on the small patch of fairly flat, low ground near the exit gate. However, she felt that the pool should be larger than that site would easily contain if it was to make a really meaningful contribution to the garden experience. She therefore decided that its surface should be extended by a certain amount of excavation into the slope to the west. To hold back the steep raw earth face which the excavation would create, she opted for the well-tried civil engineering solution of cladding it with large boulders interspaced with smaller, well-rounded rocks to form a steep beach.

Irene Shaw hoped that when garnished with a planting of ferns, ivies and hostas, with bulrush, flag and water-lilies in the water, any feeling that

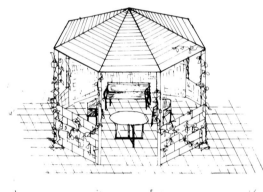

Something as simple as an octagonal structure open on five sides like the one above can make a satisfactory loggia from which to enjoy a woodland garden in poor weather. Dignifying an entrance gate by giving it a canopy provides a sense of occasion for those people passing through it while simulating the experience of walking under a tree.

men had been at work would be diminished. However, in even some of the remotest woodland areas evidence of man's activities are often revealed. Former clearings in primeval forest which have become covered by what are obviously secondary growths suggest that previously charcoal burners were at work in the area, and pits and mounds in the woodland floor betray the site of primitive mineral extraction industries, so that there is no reason why even in a natural woodland situation a pool which could have formed in a man-made pit should be offensive. In her design Irene Shaw has cleverly merged the steep rocky beach of the pool with the gravel surface of the path by setting quite sizable stone into its margin. It is a technique which she has used elsewhere on the path edges to prevent too much fine gravel from becoming tedious or to make an interesting transition between the smooth and regular paving of the loggia terrace and the gravel of the path. To enable many views over the garden to be obtained, she proposed to have solid walls on only three sides of her octagonal loggia. One side was left completely open as an entrance and the others were closed by a low stone wall.

The general surround was fencing which she specified consisted of peeled larch poles with small gaps between to lighten the general appearance. Light filtering through the fence might make the poles echo the appearance of the stems of young trees in a closely planted copse which would make the fence seem right as a woodland boundary and while being a complement to the soft landscape offer clues as to what the garden inside had to offer. Visitors would be enticed into the wood by strategically placed specimen shrubs such as the large *Pieris formosa forrestii* sited to the west of the first corner of the main path which would attract the attention of anyone entering the garden. From the point at which the *Pieris* is sited, the eye would then be lured far along the grass-mown path in the glade along the rich dark foliage of a series of *Acers* planted along its edges. This technique of drawing the eye from plant to plant has been used cleverly in many places in the garden.

Species roses and honeysuckles set to climb the stone columns of the loggia should make using it to sit and view the garden a fragrant experience and on still evenings would be likely to perfume much of the area around.

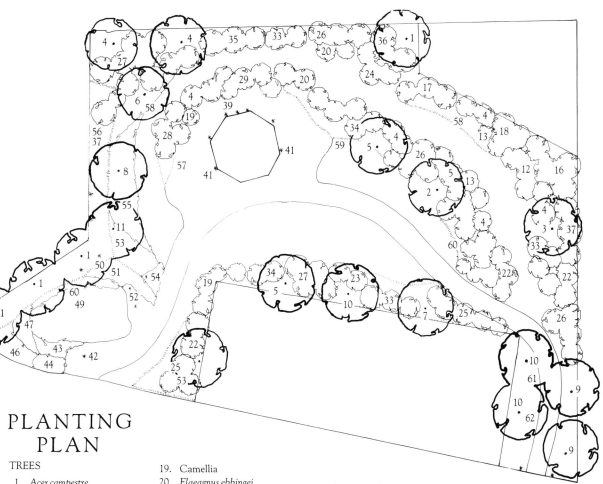

PLANTING PLAN

TREES

1. *Acer campestre*
2. *Acer griseum*
3. *Acer grosseri*
4. *Acer platanoides*
5. *Acer platanoides* 'Crimson King'
6. *Acer saccharinum*
7. *Malus floribunda*
8. *Malus* 'Profusion'
9. *Prunus avium*
10. *Sorbus aria* 'Lutescens'
11. *Tilia × euchlora*

SHRUBS

12. *Acer* 'Heptalobum'
13. *Acer japonicum*
14. *Acer palmatum*
15. *Acer palmatum* 'Atropurpureum'
16. *Acer pseudoplatanus* 'Brilliantissimum'
17. *Acer palmatum* 'Dissectum'
18. *Acer palmatum* 'Dissectum Atropurpureum'
19. Camellia
20. *Elaeagnus ebbingei*
21. *Elaeagnus pungens* 'Maculata'
22. *Enkianthus campanulatus*
23. *Mahonia aquifolium*
24. *Mahonia japonica*
25. *Osmanthus × burkwoodii*
26. *Pieris formosa forrestii*
27. Rhododendron mixed
28. *Rhus typhina*
29. *Rosa bourboniana* 'Mme Pierre Oger'
30. *Rosa centifolia* 'Fantin-Latour'
31. *Rosa damascena* 'Queen of Denmark'
32. *Salix repens argentea*
33. *Skimmia japonica rubella*
34. *Viburnum opulus*
35. *Viburnum opulus sterile*
36. *Viburnum tinus*

CLIMBERS

37. *Clematis flammula*
38. *Clematis orientalis* 'Orange Peel'
39. *Lonicera periclymenum* 'Belgica'
40. *Rosa* 'Gloire de Dijon'
41. *Rosa* 'New Dawn'

42. *Hedera canariensis*
43. *Caltha palustris*
44. *Hedera hibernica*
45. *Thelypteris limbosperma*
46. *Asplenium actiantum*
47. *Iris pseudacorus*
48. *Fyphalatifolia*
49. Waterlilies on pool
50. *Gunnera manicata*
51. *Hosta fortunei*
52. *Hedera canariensis*
53. *Primula vulgaris*
54. *Cryptogramma crispa*
55. *Lychnis flos cuculi* in meadow grass
56. *Rosa canina*
57. *Astilbe × *'Irrlicht'
58. Narcissus
59. Narcissus

60. *Geranium pratense*
61. *Hypericum hirsutum*
62. *Endymion non scripta*
63. *Betonica officinalis* in meadow grass
64. *Hypericum hirsutum*
65. *Primula vulgaris*

CHAPTER FOUR

Features in Woodland Gardens

Timber from trees felled to allow more light to reach the floor of established woodland can be used to make attractive rustic features like this seat or the risers for the flight of steps.

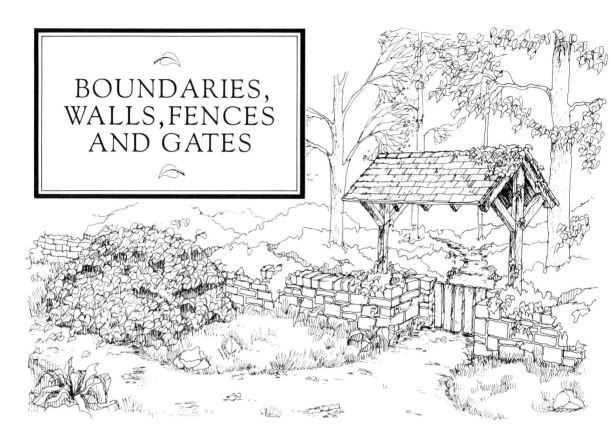

BOUNDARIES, WALLS, FENCES AND GATES

Perhaps the ideal woodland garden would extend to between 2 and 4 acres offering sufficient room for all the features and the wild and ornamental plants to be smoothly blended, but it would be small enough to be managed without too many problems. It would be sited just below the shoulder of a low hill sloping down from the north-east to the south-west. Its north and eastern boundaries would be defined by a 12 ft (3.5 m) high ancient stone or brick wall festooned with ivy, moss and ferns, and lined internally with a high hedge of evergreen trees to protect it from cold winds. There would be no obvious barrier on the south and west sides which would be protected by an unseen ha-ha wall and deep ditch allowing wonderful vistas over a beautiful rolling landscape to be fully enjoyed.

Provided that the access gates were well guarded, such a garden could be readily protected from invasion by animals like deer, hares and rabbits which, while attractive, can devastate young herbaceous plants, trees, and shrubs and make the gardening aspect of woodland gardening virtually impossible in wilder areas. Sadly, the

A solid stone wall like that shown here when well weathered and studded with trailing plants can make an incomparably beautiful boundary for any type of garden. However because they are costly these days their use has usually to be confined to the smaller woodland gardens.

ideal is rarely realisable, and the gardener's task then becomes one of making the most of the assets available.

Unless they already existed, few gardeners would be able to create the boundary defences of the type described above around a garden of that scale, although something of a similar character might be possible around a smaller plot using cheaper simulated stone to make the high walls. Otherwise, the type of perimeter barrier erected around a woodland garden will depend upon its size and the particular problems imposed by its location.

If security either from human intrusion or the invasion by damaging animals is a major consideration, a high fence of strong metal mesh supported on angle iron posts set in cement may be the only daunting choice. However, these days there are differently patterned strong metal or plastic meshes available which can make these fences seem less hostile, and happily rapid-growing evergreen and deciduous climbers like the ivies or Russian vine planted along the base line will, in two to three years, convert them into much less offensive green walls. The need for this garnishing will diminish if an irregular line of quick-growing evergreen trees is planted to hide the fence just inside the boundary.

As in many situations, the small can be the most beautiful, and as the length of the boundary decreases, it becomes less costly to provide security in ways that are aesthetically more pleasing. A palisade of half or whole unbarked or turned logs supported by a stout timber frame becomes a possibility; or, round smaller woodland gardens, the rustic atmosphere can be exaggerated by building a charming loose stone wall.

In places where security is less important, more traditional woodland fencing can be adopted. Few barriers are more attractive than the simple post and rail fence made from rough-cut unplaned timber or its more rustic version made from unbarked round posts and poles. Wattle hurdles of the type with which farmers used to make sheep pens can also make attractive and appropriately rustic woodland fences. There are also many ways of using timber for fencing arranged to form more complicated patterns, but by adopting something of this type, which is so obviously designed, gardeners must be sure that the design harmonises well with the general scheme which they are trying to develop. In a garden in which the gardener wishes to stress its rustic nature, an over-designed fence might seem over sophisticated and intrusive.

Whatever form of fence is selected, the gates set in it should always match its style. In many cases, the simple five-barred farm gate will prove the most satisfactory for main entrances with a narrower version of the same design or a simple swinging lovers' gate for purely pedestrian access. Planking picket gates, too, look well set in either post and rail or picket fences.

If a more complex patterning has been chosen for the fence, then the gate should be similarly patterned to impose harmony on the overall scheme.

Simply patterned gates made from iron bar or rod can look attractive set in walls or wooden fences, but, unless some overall very romantic Gothic atmosphere has been developed inside the garden, over-decorative ironwork for gates should be avoided.

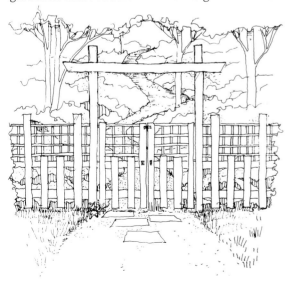

Wood, either rough cut and rustic or trimmed and smoothly planed, is clearly one of the most appropriate materials to use to make woodland gateways or boundary fences. And it is such easy material to fashion and fix that it can be used in a very wide variety of imaginative ways. Here (left) V. Amos has combined picketing and trellis to form a strong, high barrier which doesn't seem forbidding while Sonia d'A. Wright (above) by scalloping the top of a more solid fence made from rough cut timber has contrived an extremely romantic effect.

LOGGIAS AND GAZEBOS

In the widest interpretation of the term, loggias are facilities where visitors to gardens can pause to admire its views and which offer seating, shade and shelter from chilly winds or rain. Initially, gazebos (thought to be derived from the dog Latin 'I will gaze') were similar smaller buildings designed to direct attention to a rather specific and spectacular view usually beyond the garden. They were consequently often set on mounds or walls and frequently located on the margin of gardens. These days the meaning of the term gazebo has been somewhat confused, but since in purpose loggias and gazebos have much in common, in the section which follows they will be considered together.

Doric columns to support the open front and a relief sculpture set in the rear wall give this otherwise simple loggia a touch of nobility hinting that the woodland had overgrown the relics of a former civilization.

As the entrants to *The Sunday Times* Woodland Garden competition demonstrated, loggias can be as simple as a conical thatched roof held aloft on unbarked tree trunks with only the harshest of windward sides sheltered by trellis or hedging or as

Here the designer has faked the impression that the loggia is built over water by providing views of the marsh from which the stream springs from the *oeil-de-boeuf* window on one side and its course from the other. They have also ensured that the visitor will see these views because the garden path passes through the gazebo between the windows.

Low stone walls at the base of three sides of this hexagonal loggia have been used to prevent the six simple wooden columns which enclose them from seeming too leggy and insubstantial. They would also provide the structure with some useful horizontal stability.

sophisticated as miniature Greek temples with rusticated stone walls and pedimented doorways and slate or tile roofs.

Since it is one of the largest features likely to be encountered on a walk through a woodland garden, the style in which the refuge is created will impart much to the general flavour of the garden. If the gardeners take a blatantly romantic view and want to create some sort of highly cultivated version of Elysium – a leafy paradise where all man's needs, physical and mental, including stimulants to intellectual speculation, are catered for and the falsity of the situation can be deliberately ignored (the sort of place where dragons might be expected to have the temperaments of lap-dogs) – then costly and very stylish buildings would be appropriate.

However, gardeners aspiring to create a garden more attuned to nature where their own intervention has been mostly confined to enriching and gently rearranging the flora would inevitably opt for something simple, much cheaper to build, and more rustic in appearance.

Sophisticated loggias require well-trained designers and builders, whereas only moderately talented amateurs can make quite satisfactory woodland refuges for themselves. One very easy way is to modify one of the hundreds of models of workaday garden sheds which are on offer at the garden centres. Often all that is needed is the removal of the wall containing the window and the door and its replacement by a couple of stout wooden pillars to restore its structural integrity. The three remaining sides of the shed can be quickly masked by vigorous evergreen climbing plants. What is likely to be a sheet asphalt roof can be clad with wooden shingles or half-rustic poles laid closely side by side. This treatment will totally change its allure and make a splendid house for a seat with a view.

More ambitious-looking, but equally easy to build, are round, octagonal or hexagonal 'temples'. Open-sided, initially their shingle, slate or tile roofs can be supported on columns made of mellow brick, real or simulated cut stone set on broad concrete foundations or square or round sectioned timber rising from brick or stone plinths. They can be set on slabbed terraces or merely on compacted earth topped inside with gravel or coarse grit to form a floor. Lateral shelter can be provided by planting a thick evergreen hedge to shield the open windward sides, or they can be filled with trellis screening over panels of plate-glass or rigid transparent plastic sheeting.

A loggia like this with a sophisticated roof structure and ground plan is obviously a purpose built 'outdoor room' but it would be a welcoming and appropriate building to discover on a walk through a woodland garden.

A building as simple as this can make a delightful sheltered arbour without detracting in any way from the essentially rustic mood which woodland gardeners should try to create.

WATER AND BRIDGES

If there are ditches on the land in which the water runs regularly in the dry season or access to the summer water table is easy, water can be introduced to a woodland garden by excavation. In a few hours a mechanical digger can dig out the bottom of a ditch, widen it in places, or even make its course meander so that it resembles a stream. Similarly, provided ready access is available (and it might pay to ensure it), a digger can cut down into a high water table and create an attractive pond.

In circumstances where a ditch along the margins of a plot flows through land with a deep impermeable clay subsoil, it can be upgraded to become a stream linked with and feeding a pond excavated elsewhere in the garden. The golden rule to follow is to ensure that the pond to be fed is situated upstream from the ditch entrance to the feeder link. Water will then gently flood back into the pond from the stream to maintain an equal water level rather than hurrying into the pond and dropping its load of suspended sediment as its

Sophisticated arched bridges of this type over water features can look enchanting in woodland gardens. But building them is a job which should be given to experts who understand and can cater for all the loading involved.

Stream features are always more interesting if they include a change in level because water spilling over a weir introduces a happy gurgling sound to the garden.

There is always something delightful about peering down into water and it can easily be contrived by attaching transverse timbers to a pair of robust beams across a stream or pond or by simply placing stepping stones in the water.

current slows. Unless this rule is obeyed, the pond will soon become filled with sediment and quickly develop into a bog.

Gardeners who can modify ditches and create ponds by excavation are lucky. More usually they will be obliged to make artificial water features and then use guile to make them seem as natural as possible.

Fortunately, garden centres which specialise in aquatic gardeners' needs have plenty of equipment available to make that task easier. Informally shaped rigid pool liners in glass-fibre reinforced resin are available in many sizes, as are the elements necessary to make cascades and falls. Sadly, many of them are rather small-scaled to suit the needs of urban gardeners. This can be a disadvantage for woodland gardeners who obtain the best effects if they create larger ponds offering more meaningful and convincing stretches of

water. One way of overcoming this problem is to use several pond liners masking narrow gaps between them by planting tall or sprawling aquatic plants along their contiguous margins or larger gaps by making them into simulated islands supporting terrestrial plants such as small willows.

If large uninterrupted stretches of water are demanded by the design on light, well-drained land, flexible liners made from neoprene sheet which can be readily cemented or welded together are probably the most suitable. Rills and streams can be made on this land by over excavating their course to allow concrete to be used to make a continuous lining. To avoid frost damage, these linings should be reinforced with steel mesh and be at least 4 in (10 cm) but preferably 6 in (15 cm) thick. It is also possible to use pre-cast culvert units for straight reaches of streams or rills.

If the water feature is artificial, a mains feed-pipe leading to a well-disguised floating ball cock will be necessary to maintain the water level in ponds automatically. The supply of water to running features such as streams and rills will have to be maintained by recirculating their water after it has drained over a weir into an underground cistern using a submersible electric pump. It is vital that the cistern is copious, otherwise in the time taken for water pumped into the top end of the system to raise the level and make water spill over the weir back into the cistern, it might have been pumped dry.

The best bridges in woodland gardens are the simplest. Tiny streams can be bridged by a large flattish rock supported by smaller rocks on each bank or even informal stepping-stones. Heavy timbers such as railway sleepers laid side by side and supported at each end by flat-topped rocky abutments look well spanning slightly wider streams.

Fairly simple but more sophisticated timber constructions are necessary to be able to cross wider streams or ponds, and they seem to look best if their more obvious superstructures are made from rustic poles rather than finished timber.

If flints or other rocks and stones are readily available in the district, small versions of ancient hump-backed pack-horse bridges can look wonderful in a woodland setting, but it either requires a talented amateur or the services of a professional mason to make them.

PATHS AND STEPS

Paths through woodland gardens should be considered carefully. They should not be treated just as ways to get about without resorting to gum boots on wet days. They should be designed to offer visitors an adventurous and satisfying journey. If their routes are cleverly planned, they can make any garden seem much larger and by discreetly changing their direction several times the same feature seen from different places will have a distinct aspect and appear constantly unfamiliar. Thus the asset of its characteristics can be exploited several times. Although directional changes are desirable they must not, however, be too abrupt. The visitor must be coerced by fairly gentle and natural curves such as those which would be followed by a happy ambling animal rather than being bludgeoned into complying with hairpins which nature, when rampaging unbridled, rarely produces. This organic approach will lull visitors into the desirable feeling that they themselves are part of the garden rather than being unwelcome intruders. An easy way to make them change direction sharply while not being aware of the manoeuvre is to make the path enter a circular area with an object at its centre about which the path can swing before leading off in another direction.

To have their sense of adventure fully stimulated, visitors need to be provided with a new sense of normality from which to depart. This could be a fairly broad main path surfaced with packed gravel and tracking through all the major areas of the garden. It would offer the elderly firm footing and an interestingly varied journey. Branching off from the main track, and leading to more hidden areas, narrower tracks to explore could be mown for the more adventurous to follow deeper into the garden. These in their turn could branch again and where they flow under a heavier canopy they can be topped with either the very coarse gritty sand which is often encountered beneath a thick parasol of trees or softer ground bark which smells wonderfully resinous when it is

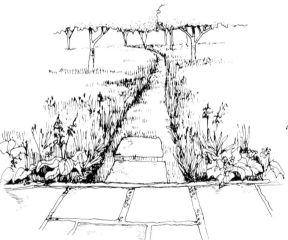

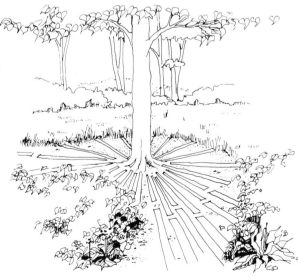

Formal paving leading to informal paving and then a mown grass path (above) will tempt visitors into exploring further into the garden.
Abrupt changes in the direction of a path seem less irritating if a tree is used as a round about. This one (near right) is made more attractive by setting radiating timbers into the gravel surface. Good dry walking can be provided by setting sections of log into the soft woodland floor (far right).

damp or when the weather is very warm. These changes in path surfaces alone can be exciting as the experience of hard gravel beneath the sole alternates with that of gently yielding turf or the muffled sound of footfalls on grit or bark.

To save the embarrassment of their having to make excuses for footprints on polished floors or carpets, the last few yards of any path leading to the house should be topped with good-looking, well-weathered formal stone slabs set in rather a casual way with some mound-forming plants inserted in the narrow gaps between them.

If formal cut stone is to be used to make steps in woodland gardens, it should be handled in an equally informal way, but once the garden has been really penetrated by a path any steps necessary to alter its level should be very informal. Using sections of log held in place by long steel pickets driven deep into the ground to form risers which hold back compacted gravel to make the treads is probably the most sympathetic way of making steps in woodlands. To prevent the top of the log risers from becoming too slippery they can have lengths of chicken wire nailed to them. While unsightly at first, these will soon disappear among an aggregation of loose gravel and leaf and twig.

Lengths of log make excellent risers for flights of steps in woodland gardens. Cladding them with wire netting nailed tightly to their top surfaces will prevent them from becoming dangerously slippery in wet weather.

FURNITURE

Since no matter whether they are made in rusting iron, poles or rough-cut timber supported on masonry or wooden columns and have their walkway paved or simple beaten earth or a gravel-topped track, pergolas will always look man-made. While enchanting features when well clad with climbing plants, if a very natural approach has been adopted to the woodland garden design, pergolas are best confined to either entrances or exits or to being used as additions to loggias where it will always be evident that man has intervened. Certainly, this was where they were sited in many of the best competition designs when entrants frequently suggested that the loggia itself should supply one of the lateral elements in the pergola support. Gardeners contemplating a more 'gardened' treatment of the theme, on the other hand, might station pergolas over a pathway elsewhere in the garden to subject visitors walking beneath it to an abrupt change in their perceptual experience to make the garden seem a more interesting or surprising place.

Apart from its use as a transparent substitute for glass in screens or as a hidden weed-suppressing sheet below gravel, plastic has no easily justified role in any well-designed garden unless it is used with such skill to simulate something else that is visually indistinguishable from the genuine material. This comment applies particularly to furniture for a woodland garden because many otherwise splendid garden designs are blemished by the seats which their owners put in them. No matter whether it is the overtly romantic or the idyllic natural aspects of a woodland garden which its design stresses the presence of brash plastic furniture will immediately destroy it.

Plain wooden seats, sagging seats of woven willow or faded cane or rustic seats constructed

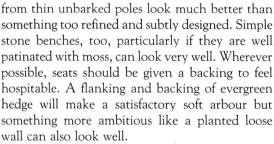

A feature like the single high quality stone vase (above) can be used to lure a visitor's attention along a path.

Suitable woodland garden seats can vary from the very rustic – like the cutaway fallen log (top left) – to the more refined cut stone bench (left). However no matter what style of seat is chosen it must be located with a suitably reassuring shelter behind and offer an interesting view.

from thin unbarked poles look much better than something too refined and subtly designed. Simple stone benches, too, particularly if they are well patinated with moss, can look very well. Wherever possible, seats should be given a backing to feel hospitable. A flanking and backing of evergreen hedge will make a satisfactory soft arbour but something more ambitious like a planted loose wall can also look well.

Wooden seats should always be stained or painted in subdued tones – dark matt greens or brown's look best in woods – although when left untreated, except with a colourless preservative, wood like pine will gradually weather to a subdued silver grey which is most attractive and natural looking.

If a seat is needed also to serve the purpose of luring the eye down a vista, something in a light-coloured stone rather than a wooden seat painted white should be chosen. The siting of seats should always be considered very carefully. They should always be stationed on a site which offers an

interesting view: over a pond, down a long vista or towards a particularly well-planted area. It also pays to remember that not everyone likes sitting fully exposed to a hot and blinding sun, so for morning and evening alike the garden needs a selection of sunny and shady seats.

Ornaments in a woodland garden should tend to the informal and be selected to interest and provoke thought at close quarters while being sited to attract attention from a distance.

Since there is no reason why a natural woodland should not have formerly sheltered ancient buildings, simulated relics made from old stone to form follies are good artefacts for attracting attention and can be both thought-provoking and, if cunningly constructed, used as a loggia or site for a seat. Rather than being shocking or controversial or very formal, the garb, attitude and subject of sculpture in a woodland garden should be casual, sylvan and bucolic, otherwise the sculpture will seem strangely alien and out of sympathy with the spirit of the place.

CHAPTER FIVE

Making a Woodland Garden

Bright clumps of flowering plants set in rough grass or
among boulders gleaming out from the shadow at the foot of a tree like these
king cups look more attractive and create a more natural mood in a woodland
garden than larger numbers of floral gems set out in cultivated beds.

The successful woodland gardeners are obliged to tread a difficult path when selecting and siting the plants which they use. While anything which they do to change the appearance of the land on which they work will introduce an element of artificiality, their aim must be to create as natural a feeling as possible. What is acceptable in this context will vary with the area in which the garden is located just as in nature natural plant populations change from region to region. Beech, horse-chestnut, birch, whitebeam and hawthorn are more usually discovered in woodlands and copses on chalky uplands than are oaks, many varieties of *Acer* or hornbeams which prefer heavy clay soils; poplars, willows and alders are the trees most often associated with wetlands.

Even if there are no trees in the potential garden at the outset, to be convincingly natural in appearance and fit snugly into the landscape, a strong matrix of appropriate species will have to be provided. Since the difference between a truly natural woodland with its limited range of varieties in a given area and a woodland garden lies in its being botanically much richer, further species will have to be selected which either harmonise or contrast happily with the more commonplace species normally found on such land.

The temptation which must be avoided is to pack the area with the most exquisite and exotic species among the varieties which will thrive in the area, for that is an approach which, although it might be acceptable in an arboretum, would tend to make a garden feel over-luxuriant and rather false. To avoid this impression, for the majority of the trees and shrubs, it is wiser to depend upon species and varieties whose leaf colour lies within the light to dark green range, only planting those with silver, yellow or dark red foliage sparsely in places where the stark contrast which they offer is useful to obtain a particular effect like luring the eye down a vista or introducing some relief into a generally green mass. By adopting this approach, the appeal of variety need not be lost, because among trees in the green range there is a wonderful choice of foliage types from the light filigree of the compound leaves of trees like the mountain ash through the simple ovals of the beech to the heavy compound palmate fronds of the chestnuts. Additional interest is engendered by the diversity

of barks and inflorescences and their following fruit which can often be quite spectacular, even in trees and shrubs whose foliage is not always very striking.

When considering plants for stocking a woodland garden, it is convenient to divide them into the roles which they are destined to play in the overall scene and within those categories to classify them on the basis of their typical form and foliage type. When analysed, a woodland consists of a 'high canopy' of tall trees which provides a

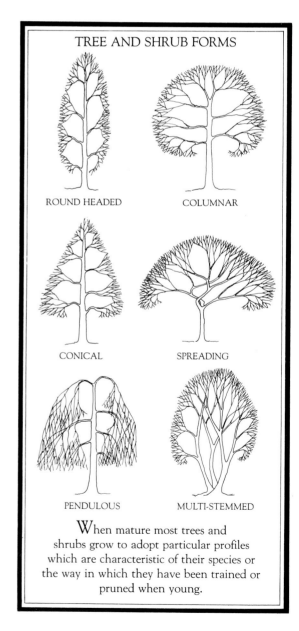

TREE AND SHRUB FORMS

ROUND HEADED   COLUMNAR

CONICAL   SPREADING

PENDULOUS   MULTI-STEMMED

When mature most trees and shrubs grow to adopt particular profiles which are characteristic of their species or the way in which they have been trained or pruned when young.

large percentage of the overhead cover and steals much of the light falling on the land. Below the high canopy there is usually an 'understorey' of smallish trees and large shrubs which are fairly shade tolerant and capable of supporting the aggressive competition of the trees for food and subsoil water supplies. A brush layer consisting of lower growing shrubs and shrubby creepers frequently develops to occupy areas of the ground between the shrubs and trees which form the understorey.

At ground level, if the overhanging parasol of foliage permits the penetration of sufficient light, there is a soft floor of herbaceous plants whose character will vary greatly, depending upon the soil conditions. On the fringes of the wood, the soft floor may be composed of those grasses and flowering plants frequently encountered at the feet of hedges in the surrounding district. Those plants will cede their place to more shade-tolerant species, or those whose annual cycle is practically accomplished before the overhanging leaf canopy has reached its summer density, the further they are sited into the wood.

In woodland areas where the drainage is poor or water remains permanently on the surface, as ponds or streams, the soft floor will be composed of marsh-loving or truly aquatic plants.

THE HIGH CANOPY

Because of the trees involved the high canopy will be the most telling feature in any woodland garden. No matter what the scale of their plot, lucky gardeners will already find them established either as components of boundary hedges or occupying a more prominent position in either their own or their neighbours' gardens. Their task could then be to increase the light penetration by thinning or in extreme cases felling some of these trees, although before any such drastic action is contemplated it is vital that they discover whether or not the trees concerned are covered by a protection order in which case in felling them the gardener would be breaking the law.

A much more enjoyable problem is in deciding what other trees should be introduced and where they should be sited to increase the high canopy and create a more typically woodland feeling. In this case both the suitability and character of the trees must be carefully considered before any decisions are made.

As mentioned previously, those trees selected to provide the obvious matrix of the garden should be, as far as possible, typical in appearance to those likely to be present in natural woodlands in the region. Since it is vital that such new introductions should establish well and grow quickly, they should also be those species well adapted to the general climate and the particular microclimate to which they will be exposed; trees which will tolerate buffeting in cold winds without their limbs being amputated or the leaves being burnt should clearly be chosen for chilly situations, while less hardy species will thrive best in their lee or given the protection of a wall.

The nature of the soil, too, must be taken into account. Even species within the same family can have quite different requirements, some enjoying moist, acid soil and others preferring dry, alkaline situations. Only when the suitability has been established should the form of trees be considered in their selection. Their most outstanding character is their shape which can vary markedly and affect the role which they can be made to play in the overall design. In general terms, the form of trees can be categorised as follows:

Columnar or fastigate forms in which a dominant upright main stem is clad with thinner erect branches for much of its length.

Round-headed forms which, when seen from afar, resemble loosely defined spheres or rough cubes of foliage held aloft on a clear main stem with possibly a few fairly obvious branches.

Conical forms in which a dominant upright main stem is clad with thinner branches which diminish in length the farther from the ground that they spring from the main stem.

Spreading forms are those in which many of the main branches tend towards the horizontal and in which the canopy is obviously much wider than it is high. Umbrella forms are a feature of trees in which the spreading characteristic of the canopy is exaggerated and made more obvious by the existence of a framework of bare spreading branches holding it aloft.

Pendulous forms are those in which the main branches and the more slender twigs curve back towards the ground as they grow. A more elegant arched version develops when initially the branches are fairly erect and then slowly arch back towards the ground.

Multi-stemmed forms usually occur by accident in nature and are eagerly sought after and dug out by nurserymen because of their charm. Several stems emerge at ground level and each carries its own head which coalesces to become a continuous wide canopy, making a single tree look like a miniature copse.

Many trees allowed to develop naturally from seed tend to start branching quite close to the surface of the ground. Nurserymen usually prune these low side branches away, only allowing branching to take place several feet above the ground when the trees become known as 'standards'. If the low branches are not removed the trees become 'feathered' and will tend to become more columnar or conical in general outline than those which have been initially shaped by pruning.

While conforming to any of the general categories designated above, the appearance of trees in the same category can vary greatly depending upon the characteristics of the foliage which they carry. Leaves can vary from being tiny little fat cushions tightly packed together like those of some conifers to the soup-plate sized, slightly lobed ovals of the empress tree which can measure more than 3 ft (1 m) across. Individually, their blades can be parallel sided or pointed, slender or stout, oval or rounded. They can be either hair-like or kidney-shaped or even circular, completely surrounding their supporting petiole. Their margins can be smooth or indented in a multitude of ways. In order to describe them precisely, botanists have given particular leaf features – such as their general shape, the form of their margins, leaf tips and leaf bases – a daunting series of names (see plant section diagram) on page 79.

But however they are described, individual leaves may be termed leaflets if they occur as components in 'compound' leaves. When borne in pairs on opposite sides of an extended petiole (leaf stalk) which terminates in a single leaflet, the

Trees and shrubs with very bright foliage are not a usual feature in most temperate woodlands and should only be used sparingly and placed with care like the one here which contrasts splendidly with the dominant dark foliage in the background and lures visitors further along the woodland path.

resulting compound leaf is described as pinnate (see diagram). If complete pinnate leaves instead of leaflets are borne on either side of the petiole, the ensemble is said to be bipinnate. A pair of oppositely attached leaflets at right angles and

close to a terminal leaflet is an arrangement known as trifoliate. A compound palmate leaf is one in which the leaflet bases spread out from a common point at the end of the petiole. A simple palmate leaf is one which is deeply and sharply indented to form a series of pointed lobes whose points would lie roughly on the circumference of a circle.

Apart from their shape, leaf colours vary greatly between species and with their development through the season. Their surface characteristics, too, can be highly distinctive. They can be rough or smooth, waxy, lightly hairy or even heavily felted, and while one surface may manifest one characteristic, the other can be quite different.

All the foliage features mentioned above, coupled with the fact that a tree's branches or foliage fronds may be tightly packed or loose and clearly separated can result in the light being defracted in different ways, causing the whole tree to be more obvious and seem larger or less noticeable and smaller. Although individual leaves may be pigmented with an identical tone of green, if their other physical characteristics differ when the trees stand side by side, their appearance will be quite different, even if their overall form and height are similar. This is another factor which must be considered when deciding on the location of trees. Other important considerations are the flowers, which may be insignificant but quite fragrant or flamboyant and scentless, followed by fruit such as bright berries, or hard and less significant nuts.

The way in which deciduous trees behave in autumn is also important. After their leaves have been nibbled into by the first frosts and they begin to die, some of them turn their departure into a joyous wake, flaring red or even sometimes a buttercup yellow or bright orange, while others make a less spectacular departure, simply browning and withering a little before they are discreetly shed. But when all the leaves of the deciduous trees have become only a wind-stirred crackling pool at their feet, the evergreens which the gardener has planted will remain to offer solace, so their shape, colour and location are very important if the garden is to remain attractive in the dead season.

USING TREES

Whether their garden is to be created on a smallish plot in the suburbs closely surrounded by other houses or on a largish tract of land in open countryside, the aim of the good woodland gardener must be to convey the impression that it is a secret and very leafy place which is only part of an area of land of similar character which stretches for miles. To maintain this illusion it is vital to mask anything beyond the boundaries, be it a view of another house or an open area of farmland. Since high formal boundary walls would suggest the unwelcome intrusion of men into an environment which should convey the impression that it had been created by nature in one of her more decorative moods, if they exist, they, too, must be hidden. By far the best way of creating perimeter sight barriers is to plant trees either alone or to hide existing walls.

To maintain the effectiveness of the barrier throughout the year without resorting to what would appear to be the unnatural process of clipping deciduous species to form a thick and twiggy hedge, the most sensible trees to use would be closely planted columnar or slender conical evergreens. Irish juniper, Leyland cypress, many of the hollies, Irish yew and many others are ideal trees for this purpose. They will tolerate close planting and tend to be well furnished with twigs and foliage right down to the ground, thus allowing no gaps to develop in the barrier. This characteristic can be fostered by discreetly pruning out overhanging branches which rob the lower branches of light in the early days and also by pruning out the leaders when the hedge has become sufficiently high to be effective.

Obviously, a good mixture of evergreens used to form the hedge would provide a more natural boundary than a long line of a single species. However, since most land boundaries are straight, to avoid their linear nature being too obvious in the winter, a good selection of evergreens of quite a different form should be planted rather haphazardly just inside the hedge line so that a clear view of its entire length can never be seen from anywhere in the garden. Plants like ponticum rhododendrons and common laurels allowed to grow unrestricted are excellent for this role.

With the decision of how to treat the boundary made, the real task of the woodland garden designer begins. No matter how small the garden, all the elements of a natural woodland should be included. In essence, they consist of very heavily planted areas where the top canopy is almost complete and the light is very subdued for most of the year with clear contrast being provided by open glades which receive plenty of sunshine for much of each bright day. Areas of well-broken light link the light and dark, creating a third environment for plants which will only tolerate a limited amount of shade.

Open water and boggy land can be found in many woodlands and should certainly be included as a fourth element in any woodland garden, while rills and small streams (real or artificially created) can meander through the boskier areas or the glades alike; ponds, if they are to be sufficiently large-scaled to be meaningful, either create their own glades or can be part of a larger glade. Room for at least some boggy land can always be found on the margins of streams or on the shores of ponds.

When designing woodland gardens it is as well to remember that just as in designing any other

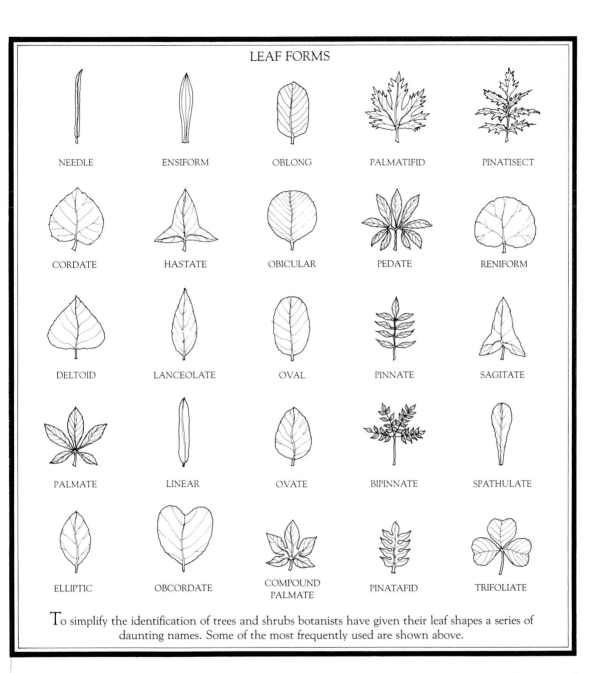

LEAF FORMS

NEEDLE ENSIFORM OBLONG PALMATIFID PINATISECT

CORDATE HASTATE OBICULAR PEDATE RENIFORM

DELTOID LANCEOLATE OVAL PINNATE SAGITATE

PALMATE LINEAR OVATE BIPINNATE SPATHULATE

ELLIPTIC OBCORDATE COMPOUND PALMATE PINATAFID TRIFOLIATE

To simplify the identification of trees and shrubs botanists have given their leaf shapes a series of daunting names. Some of the most frequently used are shown above.

type of garden or, for that matter, the decor of a room, the best effects are obtained if the design is fairly simple and uncluttered. While included with subtlety and taste so that their full contribution is not too easily understood and mentally dismissed as boring by the visitors, each element should be bold and clearly obvious when it is encountered on the garden walk. This means that in most small gardens there will only be room for the inclusion of the main typical woodland garden features – a

single meaningful glade to discover after moving well down the garden, surrounded by a single continuous band of tall canopy with areas of broken shade at its edges. A tiny rill might wander beneath the high canopy and through the broken shade, but the pond with its marshy areas would have to be located in the glade if it was to be large enough to make a significant contribution to the garden experience (see p. 122).

A small, semi-formal, sitting area close to the

house would serve to distance tall trees from most of its windows, allowing them access to plenty of light. If the area was sensitively planted around its margins it would also serve to act as something of an additional small glade, particularly if the house walls were well clad with attractive climbing plants like Virginia creeper. Moving from it through the trees which screen the large glade down the garden would increase the perception of moving from light through dark and back again into a light area, which is one of the most pleasing sensations when moving through natural woodland or the best woodland gardens.

In larger gardens there will be room for several areas of glade and bands of intervening closely planted trees. This will greatly increase the variety of experience which the woodland garden designer can offer. There can, for instance, be dry and wet glades of different sizes and there will be room for other appropriate and romantic features to discover in the deep shadow of the tall canopy – follies, ruined masonry which could be the relics of a woodman's cottage or 'natural' rocky grottos – all of which will provide additional interest. There will be more room, too, to devise baffling routes for paths through the woods which will make the garden seem even larger.

There are few hard and fast rules about the way in which trees should be used to create a tall canopy, but observation of successful woodland gardens and the role of trees in the wild suggests that particular forms are more appropriate to specific types of location.

Apart from the role in creating boundary hedges – which, incidentally, should be considered in relation to their likely effects on neighbours' views or gardens in urban and suburban situations – trees with columnar forms, because they are unusual in nature, should be used quite sparingly. Because their tall and slender shape always seems to provoke some astonishment, they can be very useful when strategically placed to lure the eye down a vista. They can also make useful building elements when creating such intriguing semi-natural features as sylvan temples. These are formed by planting columnar trees on the peri-

meter of a circle. Entering the mini-glade inside the circle always provokes a frisson of excitement. It will have a strange mystical quality because although everything seen is natural, it is obvious that man has intervened to create a sanctuary – and seeking the reason can stimulate intriguing speculation.

Trees with fairly rigid conical forms, while more frequently encountered, really only seem appropriate in the areas where they have developed naturally. They are really 'native' to many wilderness areas of the USA and northern Europe and are also frequently found at the higher altitudes elsewhere, where perhaps they look well because their conical forms echo the peaks of the mountains which surround them. But unless they are used very carefully at lower altitudes, they can seem very alien and even somewhat forbidding. This is, perhaps, a good reason for selecting only the most beautiful among them – glorious specimens like the lovely pendulous *Picea breweriana* – and placing them among a good neutral background where their shape and colour can add interest to the whole composition. In a small garden there would rarely be room for more than one such tree.

Trees with rounded heads seem to make up the majority of those encountered in nature and unless they can be viewed in isolation from some distance, their rather amorphous form when in full leaf makes them most suitable for use when massed so that their heads tend to coalesce to form a solid tall canopy. The different tones and characteristics of their leaves or the flowers and fruit which they bear can be exploited to introduce interest to the overall foliage mass.

Both spreading and pendulous trees have such distinctive forms that they demand prima donna positions, either where they are obvious at the edge of an area of tall canopy or free standing and prominent in a glade. In such situations they can often provide attractive parasols beneath which shady seats can be happily located.

Multi-stemmed trees are also too good to lose in a general mass of forest vegetation. With the several stems supporting a wide canopy they cover quite a large area of ground which can also be used to support some interesting underbrush and soft floor features, so that, when given an obvious 'solus' position, the mini copses which they make

A quintessential woodland path passing through deep shade beneath the canopy of mature acer trees to emerge in a bright sunlit glade.

can serve as a metaphor for a complete woodland acting as a stimulating aperitif, at a glance suggesting to a visitor what the whole garden is all about. Feathered trees can make a useful contribution to the understorey canopy. Because their foliage is similar to that of the high canopy, they act as a useful vertical link luring the eye upwards.

Apart from tall trees deliberately stationed in isolated positions for their ornamental effect or to mask an eye-sore beyond the garden, it is better to locate them on the outward margins of the garden, stationing smaller trees towards the edge of major pathways or glades. Trees which even when mature do not reach great heights, can also be interplanted between taller species where, together with taller shrubs, they can contribute to the understorey.

When creating both levels of foliage, species with a good mixture of foliage types should be selected to maintain interest. No area – including the least likely to be frequently visited – should ever be allowed to be completely dull, even in the depths of winter. To avoid this mistake, the use of both a variety of foliage types and the occasional inclusion of trees with more vividly coloured foliage should be carefully considered. There should always be at least one attractive evergreen and a deciduous tree with rather colourful foliage prominent somewhere along all the major sight lines in the garden.

The temptation will always be to overplant trees when making a woodland garden, but only in rare instances will it prove sensible to plant species which, when mature, become very large specimens at much less than 15–20 ft (4.5–6 m) apart. Few trees of even the smaller species should ever be planted at less than 12 ft (3.6 m) apart because it will not be long before they develop branches from the main trunk with a reach of 6 ft (1.8 m).

Following these guidelines will not present any problems for gardeners who are fortunate in having enough tall trees on the land to provide a ready-made high canopy over much of its area. They will be able to choose the cheap option of buying a few semi-mature specimens of, say, 15–20 ft (4.5–6 m) in height and many more really young trees (which are known as whips) to use for interplanting.

Gardeners obliged to make their woodlands from scratch on a cleared site will either have to be very patient or to spend much more money if their plots are not to appear rather immature and barren for many years. However, if people in this situation are willing to spend on their garden approximately what many spend on renewing their kitchens, they can buy fairly instant maturity. These days, many nurseries specialise in the supply and planting of semi-mature and genuinely mature trees of considerable stature. Four or five rather large trees, plus a dozen semi-mature trees interplanted with dozens of cheap whips can very quickly convert a smallish garden from being a barren patch of field into, if not a vast tract of woodland, at least an attractive and sizeable copse.

USING SHRUBS

Without the existence of mature trees on the site or their costly importation, apart from ultimately providing the major ingredient in the understorey, the smaller trees and taller shrubs for a few years after planting, until the tall canopy has become really effective, can offer considerable interest in what at that stage could only be called a shrub garden. They should be selected and sited below what will become or exists as the tall canopy and occasionally in a more open situation using the same criteria as those adopted when choosing the trees. The effect of their general form, leaf shape and colour and their appearance in winter should be considered in relation to the overall composition. Notable among the factors limiting the choice of many of these will be their ability to prosper in the reduced light below the tall canopy if it exists or in the broken light of the transitional areas.

Again, their likely ultimate spread will determine the distances apart at which they should be planted. There will be areas either under the tall canopy or in the transition areas between the thick wood and the open glade where dense unpenetrable thickets will be desirable. They will look natural and provide wonderful havens for the wildlife which will quickly adopt this sort of garden, even in the heart of a town. They can be made by ensuring that knowledge of the normal mature size of each species is used to plant the shrubs sufficiently close together to enable their

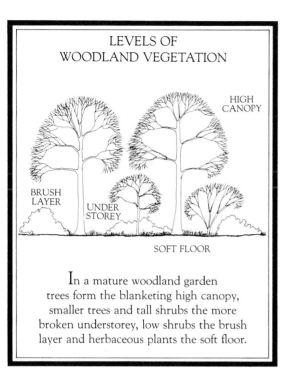

**LEVELS OF
WOODLAND VEGETATION**

HIGH
CANOPY

BRUSH
LAYER

UNDER
STOREY

SOFT FLOOR

In a mature woodland garden
trees form the blanketing high canopy,
smaller trees and tall shrubs the more
broken understorey, low shrubs the brush
layer and herbaceous plants the soft floor.

branches to tangle and their summer canopies to fuse into a single leafy mass. In open areas the design will occasionally demand the use of a single large shrub of a particular shape as a specimen feature and, of course, in this case it should be given sufficient room to be able to develop fully.

Smaller shrubs will be used singly or in clumps to simulate underbrush beneath the understorey or to create interesting feature mounds of vegetation and flowers on the soft floor of open glades. Some of the more prolific cane fruits, like the cultivated varieties of blackberry or raspberries and loganberries, can be planted to ramble wild near the edge of glades where species roses like the rugosas will also flourish.

MANAGING TREES
AND SHRUBS

Although the owners of a plot where much of the high canopy has long been established are in an enviable situation, they do face difficulties when trying to introduce further trees and shrubs to enrich the area because the established trees steal much of the water. So while all newly planted trees and shrubs should be carefully and regularly

watered in any dry spells during the first year of their life, those located within the root zone of established trees require extra special attention. They should be considered as plants isolated in pots, and daily watering in warm dry weather would not be unreasonable. When a collection of sensibly spaced large and small trees are planted simultaneously on a virgin plot, they all have an equal chance of survival and, given sufficient water, should thrive together, each having the opportunity to develop its full potential.

In both sets of circumstances, these days as well as peat the addition of expanded mineral preparations to the soil used for back filling when planting can provide a useful moisture reservoir and protect the trees and shrubs from the worst of their early water stress. Similarly, the addition of synthetic slow-release fertilisers which will feed newly planted trees and shrubs for a period of up to two years is always worthwhile.

Anyone planting up a woodland garden on a large scale should seriously consider the installation of a drip irrigation system which will take care of watering automatically at the turn of a tap. These systems are very cheap and certainly worthwhile because regularly watering a lot of trees thoroughly can be a long, cold and tedious business, and if it is done at all it must be done very well.

The need to water regularly entails other problems. The watering causes worms to concentrate in the damp soil, creating a banquet for moles. Their eager burrowing can be very disruptive to young roots which are trying hard to obtain a real foothold. The only sensible solution to the problem is to call in someone sufficiently talented and well equipped to trap them, because three or four successes may rid the garden of these pests for a full season. Only a few of them can create a terrible mess and give the impression that the whole garden is virtually overrun.

Snails and slugs, too, flourish in the damp conditions. Scandalously promiscuous, they multiply like snowflakes and can rapidly defoliate young trees. The recently introduced slug tape in which the helminthicide and bait are kept tucked safely away from other wildlife between two layers of paper which form the tape is probably the best defence against them. Strips of it can be wrapped around the main stems of trees and shrubs and a

In moist situations such as this, damp loving plants like these kingcups and astilbes make a wonderful soft floor beneath willows and acers, which also enjoy acid, boggy conditions.

branch just below the crown and if the ends of the strip are stapled together it will remain in place to be effective for several months.

Usually small young trees bought as whips and supplied either bare root or in root-balls in the late autumn become better trees more quickly than larger specimens which have been grown for a long time in a container. While some of the latter may be necessary to give some appearance of maturity at the outset the whips are likely to overtake them within five years. However, initially they are very susceptible to rabbit damage, and if these pests are a problem in the region it will always pay to protect the young trees by casing them for at least their first season inside rigid plastic tree shields. Foresters who use them claim

that not only do they fend off rabbits, they also produce some sort of screening and greenhouse effect, making the young trees grow faster than if they are exposed full frontal to chilly winds.

But no matter whether container-grown or bare-root stock is planted, it is always worth spreading black plastic over the soil surface for 18 in (45 cm) around the stem and anchoring it in place to suppress weed development in the first season. The nasty plastic can be hidden below a thick layer of more attractive ground bark.

PLANTING THE SOFT WOODLAND FLOOR

No matter whether the low vegetation is seen from woodland tracks below the shady high canopy or when strolling through the open glades, it must be established with great sensitivity if it is to retain a genuinely natural aspect while at the same time pleasing and intriguing gardeners. For the majority of them it will offer the greatest interest and the best opportunities of enjoying their hobby.

It is in this vegetation zone, too, that the aspirations of the gardener wishing to create a richly beautiful place and the conservationist wishing to ensure the survival of species meet, because even when situated in town, natural looking woodland gardens are the ideal place to offer refuge to plants threatened with extinction; some are the long-established natural species which were improved for gardeners and have fallen out of fashion and others are genuinely wildflowers which modern agriculture or land developments have put in jeopardy. Good woodland gardeners will use both classes of plant and very delicately mingle with them a few of the simpler and more attractive modern garden hybrids to brighten up and introduce more colour to particular areas.

Just as when considering the introduction of small trees and large shrubs to form the understorey, the woodland gardener will emphasise the inclusion of such species as field maples, hawthorns or goat willows which occur frequently in the landscape, only using exotic-looking subjects like magnolias or the yellow-leaved *Gleditsias* to highlight certain areas. On the woodland floor flowers found in the wild will dominate the sward. More cultivated plants such as clumps of hybrid *Hemorocallis*, *Iris germanica* or hybrid foxgloves will be used sparingly to introduce further colour and interest and to make the distinction between attempting to simulate a wilderness and gardening.

Because it involved a long programme of collecting seeds from the wild, producing a soft floor for a woodland garden which was really convincing was a difficult task in the past. Fortu-

nately, however, these days both institutions and commercial seed companies have made it much easier. Several of them are growing wildflowers as they would any other seed crop or multiplying them vegetatively as would any other nurseryman. The business has now become so sophisticated that specialist wildflower seed merchants can supply seed mixtures suitably balanced to make them appropriate in particular situations, whether they be dry and open or damp and shady, and on acid or alkaline soil. Perennial or biennial wildflowers can also often be obtained as young containerised plants ready for planting to begin flowering in the same season. When seed mixtures are obtained, they usually contain a high proportion of grass seed which will help to produce a quick ground covering sward and offer the wildflowers both the protection and competition which they seem to need to thrive.

By virtue of their ability to offer higher light intensities, it is on the more open woodland edges and in the glades that flower meadows can make their most colourful displays for the longest periods each year. Although hundreds of species of wildflower are available as seed, as few as nine of

A carpet of wildflowers like cowslips, daisies and dandelions among tussocky grass can be quickly produced by deliberately sowing wildflower meadow seeds mixtures.

those which occur commonly will ensure that the meadow is a bright picture from spring right through to the autumn in temperate climate.

⌒Cowslips with a maximum height of only 6–9 in (15–22 cm) have bright green rosettes of single leaves and can carry up to twenty heads of pale yellow flowers in spring. Their flowers also make fine wine.

⌒Ox-eye daisy grows up to 3 ft (1 m) and has a delicate filigree of foliage and astonished-looking white daisy heads in early summer.

⌒Ragged robin, 2 ft (60 cm) tall with narrow-leaved foliage, is topped by drifts of mauve flowers which become a Mecca for bees a week or two later.

⌒The mid-blue, bell-shaped, flowers of delicate little 9 in (22 cm) harebells nod charmingly among the grass from early to late summer.

⌒From early to high summer simple mauve flowers splash the thick 1½–2 ft (45–60 cm) mounds of handsome palmate meadow cranesbill foliage with a froth of colour.

⌒The pea-like shrubby foliage of spiny rest-harrow will rise to 1 ft (30 cm) and carry attractive pink flowers from midsummer until early autumn and will be shunned by cats who find it loathesome.

⌒Butterflies, on the other hand, seem to love the masses of purplish flowers carried at 2½ ft (76 cm) between midsummer and the autumn above the handsome basal rosettes of deeply cut leaves of the greater knapweed.

⌒In the late summer and autumn, as though in defiance of the stage of the season, lady's bedstraw offers a reprise of spring with its jaunty yellow show of flowers on 1 ft (30 cm) spikes.

⌒The 18 in (45 cm) tall umbrella-headed white flowers of burnet-saxifrage carried above delicate fern-like foliage will continue to offer their enchantment from late summer well into the autumn.

With the single exception of the cowslip, all these can be raised from seed broadcast or sown directly into patches of cultivated soil in early spring. However, in the latter case most of them will not flower in the first year. Alternatively, the seed can be sown individually, indoors, in late winter in small pots of John Innes No 1 compost. This will produce robust plants for planting out in late spring, a few of which may bloom in their first season.

Cowslips are best sown into patches of cultivated soil in the autumn and then thinned out late in the following spring. Unlike cultivated species, wildflowers have the great advantage that they need no feeding if they are to prosper. Most meadow wildflowers which seed prolifically can be established by sowing on well spaced patches of cultivated soil and infilling between the patches with a simple grass mixture. In a year or two, self-sown seed will extend the flowers to much of the meadow area. This is probably the best insemination technique to employ when establishing a woodland garden on a new site.

In gardens in which mature trees and shrubs and lawns have long been established and the gardener's job is to intensify the planting, wildflowers can best be established by allowing the lawn to naturalise by greatly reducing the mowing regime over most of the area and cutting out 1 sq yd (1 m²) patches of turf at intervals to provide sites for sowing the wildflower seed or planting out clumps of biennial or perennial plants.

Apart from possibly keeping a small area of lawn near the house close mown, the rest of the area should only be mown very lightly in late spring after the spring flowers have matured and shed their seed and more thoroughly in late autumn to tidy areas for the winter.

As the canopy develops in the more heavily wooded areas, the shade below will gradually become invaded by those plants which most appreciate those conditions. However, the gardener can do much to establish ground-covering plants under these conditions. While some of them, including the shade-tolerant grasses like *Holcus lanatus*, will develop well from seed, quicker effects are often obtained by introducing young plants. The yellow dead-nettle *Lamium galeobdolon* or the neater magenta-pink-flowered *Lamium maculatum* are very easy to establish and

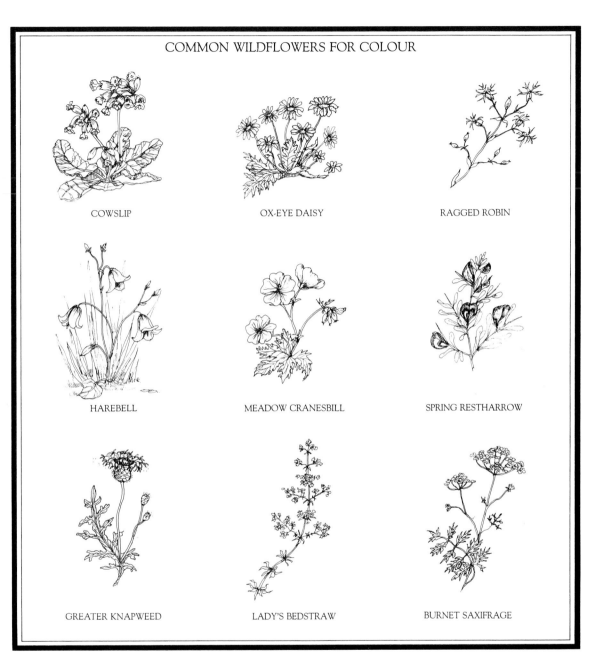

COMMON WILDFLOWERS FOR COLOUR

COWSLIP

OX-EYE DAISY

RAGGED ROBIN

HAREBELL

MEADOW CRANESBILL

SPRING RESTHARROW

GREATER KNAPWEED

LADY'S BEDSTRAW

BURNET SAXIFRAGE

spread very quickly if a short length of stem with some roots attached is simply pressed into a patch of soil disturbed with a hand-fork. The lesser and greater periwinkle, Irish ivy, and wild strawberries, also respond well to this casual treatment.

Better planting holes and more attention – particularly watering – after planting are needed to ensure the establishment of a range of more spectacular plants which will enjoy full shade. If they are happy, the bugles, particularly the evolved selections like *Ajuga reptans* 'Atropurpurea', with its metallic reddish purple leaves, will soon form a solid carpet. Species spurges like *Euphorbia robbiae*, saxifrages like S. *fortunei*, the blue forget-me-not flowered *Brunnera macrophylla* and shy wood violets provide more erect features to give the soft floor more vertical character when planted in telling clumps.

Given the broken shade on the edges of glades and pathways, the range of planting possibilities widens, particularly as these conditions favour many of the garden species and hybrids which look well in woodland situations

A host of the more subdued hostas, hypericums, bergenias, epimediums, pulmonaria, hellebores, alchemillas, astilbes, foxgloves, irises like *I. foetidissima* and *I. pseudacorus*, lychnis, several species of lily, nicotianas and astrantrias enjoy partial shade. An interesting range of ferns also look particularly appropriate on woodland fringes.

No mention has yet been made of the bulbs and corms which make our woodlands so beautiful in spring and their glades so attractive later in the year and certainly no woodland garden should be without them. Under the thickest canopy bluebells, snowdrops and scillas will flourish and spread quickly, hurrying through the most significant parts of their life-cycles before the deciduous trees develop most of their leaves.

Some of the earlier flowering and simpler narcissi can also be naturalised in the heart of the wood and they also look wonderful fringing its edges. Muscaris and cyclamens, particularly the smaller species, will also flourish in partial shade.

Glade areas can have their soft floor beautifully enriched by planting the bulbs of a host of plants which enjoy plenty of sunshine. Although there is always a risk that this could result in them appearing rather unnatural, they will always have a strong appeal for the incurably romantic and if the bulbs are selected with care they will be able to guarantee the presence of bright flowers throughout the season.

A great many bulbs like allium, crocus, colchicum, sternbergia, anemone, chionodoxa, winter aconite, the small fritillaries and species gladioli are readily available from specialist small bulb suppliers. When poring over their catalogues the aim should be to isolate the less flamboyant varieties which, while brightening glades, will allow them to develop and retain a natural if idyllic feeling. The general rule in planting them is that their tips should be covered by a depth of soil equivalent to their maximum length and that they should be firmly bedded in so that there are no air gaps between the edge of the bulb and the more consolidated soil surrounding the planting hole.

PLANTING THE WATER MARGINS

The water features with their surrounds provide one of the most exciting areas for gardening in woodland gardens, but, because plants thrive so well in water or damp soil, gardeners must exercise great restraint otherwise the lovely natural quality of these areas will be lost. The simpler and smaller paler coloured water-lilies, for example, are more

Running water creates too turbulent conditions to enable water lilies to thrive but stream edges offer splendid moist conditions for the growth of bog plants which prosper so well that they tend to gigantism.

suitable than the large and more exotic hybrids.

The temptation to create a gravelly dry area above the water level to be able to contrast dry and moisture-loving plants, while an attractive idea in many gardens, could appear very contrived in a woodland garden. However, these constrictions are not a very limiting burden for really imaginative gardeners because there are plenty of wonderful plants available to use in a truly natural pond or marginal situation. Fine small plants which enjoy boggy sites are marsh marigolds, the astilbes, sedges, marsh gentians, grasses like Yorkshire fog and the molinias, Siberian irises, the dwarf meadowsweets, *Primula denticulata* and globe flowers. Among many good medium-sized damp lovers are water avens, day lilies, *Iris kaempferi*, yellow loosestrife, Rodgersias, candelabra primulas and spiderworts.

In large gardens American skunk cabbages, peltiphyllums, ornamental rhubarb and *Gunnera manicata* can be used to make really bold effects. Beautiful pink cardamines, golden and variegated sedges, *Iris laevigata*, reedmace and spearwort relish having their roots in mud or the very shallow water of pond or stream fringes. Water of between 6 in (15cm) and 12 in (30cm) deep makes a better home for species like sweetflag, pickerell weed and arum lilies.

Apart from the water-lilies, buck bean, Cape pondweed and arrowheads are among the most attractive of the species which enjoy really deep water of more than 1 ft (30 cm) deep. To be able to control them, it is better to plant them into a rich loam confined in hessian set inside submerged baskets which can be removed from time to time when they become overcrowded and the plants are ready to be divided.

One of the most delightful woodland garden features is a moss lawn which can be developed on the damp verge of a pool well overhung and shaded by trees and rarely touched by sunlight.

Moss and liverworts will also transform sections of rotting logs into charming features if the decaying wood is placed in shady situations where it will never dry out. When its moss cladding has developed, this type of feature will offer a specially protected microclimate in its lee where a small plant like a violet or a primula would prosper and look extra beautiful against the mossy background. An overhanging fern frond would provide a fine frame for this sort of growing plant arrangement. One great advantage of woodland gardens is that they offer endless opportunities for making the sort of compositions which Dürer so enjoyed drawing.

MANAGEMENT

It would be misleading to suggest that woodland gardens remain attractive places throughout the year without management. Those extra vigorous plants, which we term weeds rather than wildflowers, like nettles, for example, look splendid when they are bright green, young and succulent bursting away from the earth in the spring, but they have little appeal when they have matured and collapsed in a half-rotting heap after a late summer storm. While a few in an odd corner might be welcome, like brambles they will need carefully controlling, because if you have a few one year, like rabbits you will have many the next.

Since the careless use of weed-killers would put the beautiful wildflowers at risk, controlling the real weeds has to be accomplished by carefully cutting them out using a sickle and secateurs. In the case of brambles, some further control can be obtained without too much risk by painting the cut stems where they emerge from the ground with brushwood killer. On still days it would also be possible to spray weed-killer on to thick blankets of nettles, making a solid cover over the ground without endangering surrounding plants or little gems which may be developing below the nettle canopy. Clearly, however, when starting a woodland garden on a bare site there is a good case for making serious attempts to eradicate the worst of the more aggressive perennial weeds like ground elder, docks, nettles and brambles before serious sowing and planting begins. In either new or old gardens which are being modified, when introducing clumps of herbaceous plants or even trees and shrubs to inseminate the 'wild', for at least two seasons until they are well established and can compete on their own, they must be given their own surrounding weed-free zone. Planting them through black plastic sheeting topped with coarse grit, gravel or a thick layer of ground bark to suppress weeds or make them much easier to pull out is the only alternative to constant vigilance and removing the weeds by hand when they are first noticed.

In essence, woodland gardening involves giving nature her head while always keeping her gently in check. This can include managing the light by pruning away light-thieving fronds of trees forming the high canopy, to allow small trees and shrubs forming the understorey to become well established and develop a good shape.

Normally, it is better to consider areas far from the house as true wilderness in which the gardener rarely intervenes while gardening more positively the nearer the house is approached, because there is something a bit daunting and claustrophobic about feeling that the house is about to be engulfed. A feeling of reassurance might be

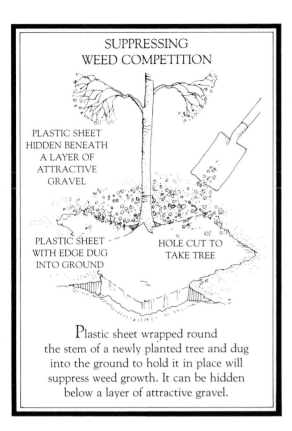

SUPPRESSING WEED COMPETITION

PLASTIC SHEET
HIDDEN BENEATH
A LAYER OF
ATTRACTIVE
GRAVEL

PLASTIC SHEET
WITH EDGE DUG
INTO GROUND

HOLE CUT TO
TAKE TREE

Plastic sheet wrapped round
the stem of a newly planted tree and dug
into the ground to hold it in place will
suppress weed growth. It can be hidden
below a layer of attractive gravel.

provided by a small area of mown lawn outside the windows and a flower bed or two. But the overall visual impression should be that nothing is too orderly – no beds packed with picture postcard annuals but rather traditional plants and flowers which are said to offer a better quality of nectar for the bees.

While mowed, the lawn must not appear too manicured, hedges should be thick but not obviously clipped and the bases of shrubs and trees should be allowed to frill enthusiastically. This approach will help a woodland garden to become a meaningful wildlife conservation area where insects, amphibians, small mammals and birds can find a safe home and where no attempt should be made to curb their activities unless it becomes obvious that they could lead to the permanent demise of cherished plants. Then, although it may sound like heresy, the only satisfactory solution may be to resort to the careful and selective use of those chemicals which are least likely to do long-term damage to the environment. To anyone who has witnessed the pace at which green- and black-flies, an attack of red spider mites or a plague of saw-

fly caterpillars can devastate and frequently kill outright young plants, the idea of being able to control them by picking them off by hand or banishing them with a dousing in washing-up water is patently ludicrous. Fortunately, these days there are several very effective, selective and non-persistent pesticides available which can provide solutions without damaging the general environment.

When a rich woodland garden has become established and is being managed properly, plants like honesty will be allowed to seed everywhere, providing nectar for adult orange-tip butterflies whose larvae thrive on the leaves of cuckoo flower and Jack-by-the-hedge. Ice plants, lavender, perennial sweet pea, buddleia, honeysuckle, antirrhinums and roses like Albertine provide feasts for a host of insects.

Apart from its fishy denizens, which seem to arrive whether introduced by man or not, large ponds and their surrounds quickly become wildlife havens. Skyscraper bulrushes reflected in their smooth water provide cosy nesting for ducks, moorhens, coots and dabchicks. Elsewhere goldfinches, siskins and bullfinches will show off their acrobatics to snatch seed from the giant parasols of hogweed, while harvest mice convert reeds into high-rise apartments. In the secluded sanctuary of their undergrowth shy, rare bitterns find a perfect retreat.

In high summer insect life in a pond region can become truly frenzied. Large and small whites, peacocks, small tortoiseshells and wallbrown butterflies convert thick drifts of soft mauve, great hairy willow-herb into a kaleidoscope of colour, and later, when its seed is ripe, it makes a great attraction for birds.

Using more erect plants as a natural trellis, field bindweed covers the ground with a green mattress which fairly throbs with life. The buzz of bees pillaging nectar from its white bell flowers would shame a hive, while in the sauna-damp gloom below the leaves, frogs, toads and newts luxuriate.

One of the conservation gardener's most important tasks is to ensure that there are plenty of rich nectar-producing flowers because there is no point whatsoever in providing lush foliage on which caterpillars can chew and get fat if there is nothing for them to eat when they metamorphose into beautiful butterflies.

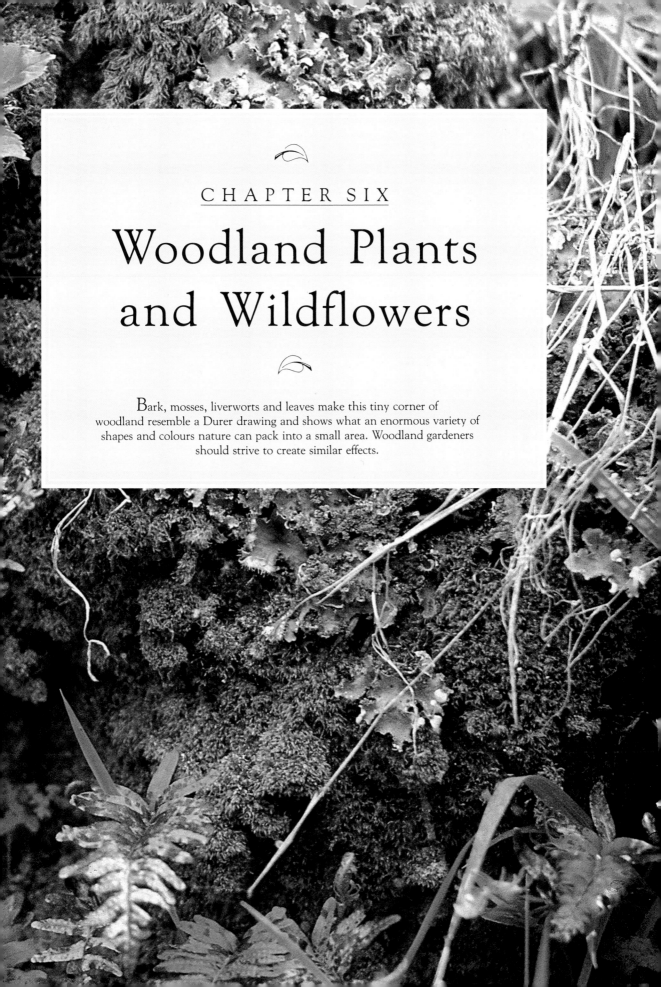

CHAPTER SIX

Woodland Plants and Wildflowers

Bark, mosses, liverworts and leaves make this tiny corner of
woodland resemble a Durer drawing and shows what an enormous variety of
shapes and colours nature can pack into a small area. Woodland gardeners
should strive to create similar effects.

The plants listed in the following tables are mostly hardy and suitable for growing on a wide range of soil types provided they are adequately drained. They have been selected because they are the type of plants which look well in woodland or woodland margin situations.

The lists should merely be treated as a guide to what is available to woodland gardeners and used to aid preliminary plant selection. Before final decisions are made, further information should be sought in specialist books devoted to particular types of plants – trees, shrubs, herbaceous perennials, etc. This is essential to ensure that the right plant is chosen for planting in each situation. Although the plants in these lists have been divided according to the type of light they prefer, there are few hard and fast rules. Plants frequently amaze by their good performance in what appear to be abnormal situations; sometimes, perhaps, because while certain conditions seem unfavourable, good growth is encouraged by other factors such as a rich soil which is ideal for them but not immediately obvious.

TREES

S = less than 20 ft (6 m) when mature   M = over 20 ft (6 m) when mature   T = over 40 ft (12 m) when mature

Evergreen trees which tolerate heavy shade

LATIN NAME	COMMON NAME	SIZE	FORM	DESCRIPTION
Buxus sempervirens	Common box	S	Bushy	Small dark green oval leaves
Laurus nobilis	Sweet bay	S	Bushy	Shiny dark green oval leaves
Ligustrum vulgare	Common privet	S	Bushy	Shiny dark green small oval leaves
Picea breweriana	Brewer's weeping spruce	T	Conical, pendulous	Dark blue-green needles on trailing branchlets
Quercus ilex	Holm oak	T	Broad domed	Dark green shiny leaves; greyish below

Evergreen trees which tolerate half shade

Arbutus unedo	Strawberry tree	S	Loose	Narrow oval dark green leaves; orange fruit
Cedrus atlantica glauca	Blue cedar	T	Conical	Blue-grey needle-like leaves
Cedrus atlantica glauca 'Pendula'	Weeping blue cedar	T	Pendulous	Blue-grey needle-like leaves
Cedrus deodara	Himalayan cedar	T	Conical	Dark green tufts of needles
Chamaecyparis nootkatensis 'Pendula'		M	Pendulous	Dark green fleshy packed leaflets
Cryptomeria japonica 'Elegans'		M	Bushy	Finely divided furry foliage

LATIN NAME	COMMON NAME	SIZE	FORM	DESCRIPTION
Cupressus glabra 'Conica'	Arizona cypress	T	Narrow, conical	Blue-grey cypress foliage
Ilex cornuta		S	Bushy	Rectangular spined leaves; red fruit
Ilex crenata 'Convexa'	Japanese holly	S	Bushy	Small glossy puckered leaves; black berries
Juniperus communis 'Hibernica'	Irish juniper	M	Columnar	Prickly short leaves with silvery undersides
Juniperus conferta	Shore juniper	S	Very low spreading	Bright apple green prickly foliage
Juniperus horizontalis 'Glauca'	Blue creeping juniper	S	Very low spreading	Whipcord branches of steely blue foliage
Magnolia grandiflora	Evergreen magnolia	M	Loose, spreading	Large shiny leaves; large waxy cream blooms
Nothofagus dombeyi		M	Loose, bushy	Small doubly toothed dark green leaves
Pinus ponderosa	Ponderosa pine	T	Narrow, conical	Long dark green needles on drooping branches
Pinus sylvestris	Scots pine	T	Irregular	Long grey needles on loose branches

Deciduous trees which tolerate shade

Corylus maxima 'Purpurea'	Filbert	S	Erect, shrubby	Distinct purple foliage; catkins and nuts
Crataegus monogyna	Common hawthorn	S	Erect, shrubby	Small palmate dark green leaves; white flowers; red berries
Fraxinus excelsior 'Pendula'	Weeping ash	M	Pendulous	Pinnate leaves on drooping twigs
Sambucus racemosa 'Plumosa Aurea'	Golden cut-leaf elder	S	Loosely bushy	Deeply cut golden foliage; white flowers; black berries

Deciduous trees which tolerate half shade

Acer griseum	Paper bark maple	M	Loose, domed	Scaling cinnamon-coloured bark; green leaves; red in autumn
Acer pensylvanicum		M	Loose, domed	Three-lobed green leaves; yellow in autumn; green and white striped bark
Aesculus hippocastanum	Horse-chestnut	T	Tall and bushy	Palmate green leaves; cream flower candles
Betula jacquemontii	Himalayan birch	M	Broadly conical	Dazzling white bark; leaves red in autumn

Appropriately named *Magnolia stellata* offers a dazzling canopy of white starlike flowers in the spring.

DECIDUOUS TREES WHICH TOLERATE HALF SHADE

LATIN NAME	COMMON NAME	SIZE	FORM	DESCRIPTION
Betula pendula 'Youngii'	Weeping birch	M	Pendulous	Small green leaves; gold in autumn
Castanea sativa	Sweet chestnut	T	Broad, domed	Glossy palmate leaves; chestnuts follow catkins
Cercidiphyllum japonicum	Katsura tree	M	Spherical	Bright pink to sea green heart-shaped leaves
Corylus avellana	Hazel	S	Bushy	Oval green leaves; yellow in autumn; catkins and nuts
Cydonia oblonga	Common quince	M	Loose, domed	Oval green leaves; yellow in autumn; golden-yellow fruit
Elaeagnus angustifolia	Bohemian olive	S	Loose, bushy	Silver foliage; amber oval 'olives'
Fagus sylvatica	Common beech	T	Erect, domed	Silver bark; clear green oval veined leaves
Ginkgo biloba	Maidenhair tree	T	Erect, loosely columnar	Fan-shaped leaves with prominent veins; butter yellow later
Gleditsia triancanthos	Honey locust	M	Loose, domed	Bright green feathery leaves; yellow in autumn
Laburnum alpinum	Scotch laburnum	S	Parasol, domed	Bright green leaves; chains of gold flowers
Larix decidua 'Fastigata'	Fastigate common larch	M	Erect, columnar	Fine leaves form bright green tufts along twigs
Liquidamber styraciflua	Sweet gum	T	Loose, erect	Five to seven lobed shiny green leaves; crimson in autumn
Liriodendron tulipifera	Tulip tree	T	Loose, erect	Palmate leaves; butter yellow in autumn; yellow-green tulip flowers, orange inside
Magnolia stellata	Star Magnolia	S	Loose, bushy	Oval mid-green leaves; starlike white flowers
Malus 'Evereste'	Crab apple	S	Loose, erect	Pink-tinged flowers; vivid red fruit
Malus 'Golden Hornet'	Crab apple	M	Loose, erect	White flowers; spectacular yellow fruit
Malus 'John Downie'	Crab apple	M	Loose, erect	White flowers; orange and scarlet fruit
Metasequoia glyptostroboides	Dawn redwood	T	Conical	Feathery plume-like foliage; bright green/golden in autumn
Nyssa sylvatica		M	Broad, columnar	Pointed oval dark glossy green leaves; red/orange/yellow in autumn
Populus alba	White poplar	T	Erect, domed	White-woolly underleaves; yellow in autumn

DECIDUOUS TREES WHICH TOLERATE HALF SHADE

LATIN NAME	COMMON NAME	SIZE	FORM	DESCRIPTION
Populus tremula	Aspen	T	Erect, domed	Green toothed trembling leaves; butter yellow in autumn; catkins
Prunus subhirtella 'Pendula Rubra'		M	Parasol, domed	Green oval leaves; rose pink blossom
Pyrus salicifolia 'Pendula'	Weeping pear	S	Pendulous	Thin leaves covered with silky down; white flowers
Quercus coccinea splendens		T	Loose, domed	Deeply lobed leaves; scarlet in autumn
Quercus robur	Common oak	M	Loose, domed	Lobed leaves; dark green above; light below; acorns
Robinia pseudoacacia	False acacia	M	Loose, domed	Bright green oval leaflets; white flowers
Salix alba	White willow	T	Erect, loose	Silky silver-green leaves; catkins
Salix babylonica	Weeping willow	M	Pendulous	Narrow green leaves; bluish below; catkins
Salix caprea	Goat willow	S	Shrubby	Oval green leaves; grey below; catkins
Salix fragilis	Crack willow	M	Domed	Glossy dark green leaves; bluish below; catkins
Sorbus aucuparia vilmorinii	Mountain ash	S	Loose, erect, domed	Pinnate leaves; cream flowers; orange-red berries
Syringa vulgaris	Lilac	S	Loose, bushy	Oval bright green leaves; white/mauve/pink/purple flowers
Stewartia sinensis		S	Shrubby	Green foliage turns rich gold in autumn; white flowers
Zelkova serrata		M	Spreading	Grey flaky bark; green foliage flares bronze-red in autumn

Deciduous trees preferring open situations

Cercis siliquastrum	Judas tree	M	Loose, erect	Green heart-shaped leaves; lilac flowers
Cornus florida	Flowering dogwood	M	Bushy	Oval green leaves; white flowers
Cornus nuttallii	Nuttalls dogwood	M	Open sphere	Oval green leaves; red in autumn; white flowers
Davidia involucrata	Handkerchief tree	M	Domed, conical	Shiny bright green leaves; paler below; white flowers
Parrotia persica		S	Spreading	Large deep green leaves; high coloured in autumn; red flowers

SHRUBS

S = below 5 ft (1½ m)   M = 5–10 ft (1½–3 m)   T = 10 ft plus (3 m)

Evergreen shrubs which tolerate shade

LATIN NAME	COMMON NAME	SIZE	FORM	DESCRIPTION
Arundinaria murielae	Bamboo	M	Arching clumps	Bright green foliage, fading to yellow
Arundinaria nitida	Bamboo	M	Arching clumps	Lush green, purple striped leaves
Camellia japonica 'Adolphe Audusson'		M	Compact	Glossy dark green leaves; semi-double deep red flowers
Camellia japonica 'Marguerite Gouillon'		M	Bushy	Glossy dark green leaves; pink flowers striped deep pink
Camellia × williamsii 'Donation'		T	Erect	Glossy dark green leaves; semi-double pink flowers
Danae racemosa	Alexandrian laurel	S	Erect	Shiny dark narrow leaves; red berries
Garrya elliptica		T	Erect	Shiny oval leaves; notable catkins
Hypericum calycinum	St John's wort	S	Mound	Fresh green oval leaves; yellow cup flowers
Kalmia latifolia	Calico bush	T	Loose, bushy	Large dark green glossy oval leaves; bright pink flowers
Mahonia × 'Charity'	–	M	Erect, loose	Large dark green pinnate leaves; chains of yellow flowers
Pieris 'Forest Flame'		M	Erect, bushy	Foliage changes from red through pink to dark green; white flowers
Viburnum tinus	Laurustinus	T	Erect, bushy	Shiny dark green oval leaves; white flowers

Evergreen shrubs which tolerate half shade

Olearia macrodonta	New Zealand holly	M	Erect	Holly-like dark green leaves; white daisy-like flowers
Rhododendron arboreum		T	Erect, loose	Prominently veined leaves, green above, red below; white to blood red flowers
Rhododendron cinnabarinum		T	Erect, loose	Attractive bark; red flowers; scaly leaves

EVERGREEN SHRUBS WHICH TOLERATE HALF SHADE

LATIN NAME	COMMON NAME	SIZE	FORM	DESCRIPTION
Rhododendron yunnanense		T	Erect, loose	Dark green lanceolate leaves; pink flowers
Rosmarinus officinalis 'Miss Jessop's Variety'	Rosemary	S	Bushy	Small dark green leaves; thickly clad twigs; blue flowers
Senecio greyi		S	Mound	Soft rounded silver leaves; bright yellow daisy-like flowers
Yucca filamentosa		S	Spiky clump	Spiky rosettes of shiny leaves; panicles of cream flowers

Evergreen shrubs which need an open situation

Lavandula spica	Old English lavender	S	Bushy	Silver-grey dissected leaves; blue flower spikes.

Deciduous shrubs which tolerate heavy shade

Aralia elata	Japanese angelica	M	Erect	Huge light green compound leaves; white flower panicles
Fuchsia riccartonii	Hedging fuchsia	M	Erect	Mid-green oval leaves; pendant scarlet flower bells
Hydrangea macrophylla 'Blue Wave'	Lace-cap hydrangea	T	Erect	Bold bright green leaves; blue composite flowers
Hydrangea sargentiana		T	Erect, loose	Large velvety leaves; bluish and white florets
Spiraea × arguta 'Bridal Wreath'		S	Bushy	Leaves resemble maidenhair fern; white flowers
Spiraea × bumalda 'Anthony Waterer'		S	Bushy	Cream-tipped, pink-edged leaves; carmine pink flower spikes
Spiraea × bumalda 'Gold Flame'		S	Bushy	Bright gold leaves; crimson flower spikes
Symphoricarpos doorenbosii	Snowberry	M	Bushy	Bright green rounded leaves; pearly white berries

Rhododendrons are among the most successful evergreen shrubs which will tolerate half shade and provide vivid colour.

Deciduous shrubs which tolerate half shade

LATIN NAME	COMMON NAME	SIZE	FORM	DESCRIPTION
Acer palmatum 'Dissectum Ornatum'		T	Spreading	Very finely cut, fresh green foliage; bronzy yellow in autumn
Amelanchier canadensis	Snowy mespilus	T	Spreading	Pink- to copper-coloured foliage; clusters of small white flowers
Buddleia alternifolia	Butterfly bush	T	Loose, arching	Thin willowlike foliage; massed tiny purple florets
Buddleia globosa	Orange ball tree	T	Loose, arching	Long oval strongly veined leaves; tangerine florets in spherical clusters
Clerodendrum trichotomum		M	Erect	Mid-green shiny oval leaves; clusters of white flowers
Cytisus × praecox	Broom	S	Arching, mound	Small pale green leaves; pale cream flowers
Daphne mezereum	Daphne	S	Erect	Fresh green small leaves; starlike mauve flowers
Deutzia × lemoinei		T	Arching	Thin oval leaves; clusters of white single flowers
Eucryphia glutinosa		T	Erect	Pinnate foliage; large white flowers, conspicuous stamens
Exochorda racemosa		M	Arching	Clusters of large single white flowers with dark eyes
Philadelphus × virginalis 'Virginal'	Mock orange	M	Erect, bushy	Mid-green leaves; double white flowers
Potentilla fruticosa 'Veitchii'		M	Bushy	Bright green leaves; white single flowers
Rhododendron occidentale		T	Loose, erect	Glossy green leaves; pink/yellow/scarlet in autumn; pink to orange flowers
Rhus typhina 'Laciniata'	Sumach	T	Loose, erect	Large finely dissected leaves; orange in autumn; crimson fruit spikes
Rosa moyesii		T	Arching	Loose blood-red single blooms
Rosa mundi		M	Shrubby	Blooms have pink and white splashes on crimson ground
Rosa rubrifolia		M	Shrubby	Plum grey foliage; small single pink blooms
Rosa rugosa		M	Shrubby	Apple green foliage; single crimson blooms
Rosa 'Emanuel'		M	Shrubby	Blush-pink blooms with gold-tinted petal base
Rosa 'Frühlingsgold'		M	Bushy	Large golden-yellow single blooms

LATIN NAME	COMMON NAME	SIZE	FORM	DESCRIPTION
Rosa 'Graham Thomas'		M	Very bushy	Cupped 'Old Rose' blooms in glistening yellow
Rosa 'Grouse'		S	Spreading	Ground cover with semi-double soft pink blooms
Rosa 'Heritage'		M	Shrubby	Cup-shaped shell-pink blooms
Rosa 'Lucetta'		M	Arching, bush	Large semi-double blush-pink blooms
Rosa 'Mary Rose'		M	Very bushy	Many petalled pink damask-type blooms
Rosa 'Partridge'		S	Spreading	Ground cover with translucent white single blooms
Rosa 'Penelope'		M	Shrubby	Glossy leaves and trusses of creamy-pink blooms
Rosa 'Pheasant'		S	Spreading	Ground cover with deep, rose-pink double blooms
Rosa spinosissima	Scottish burnet	S	Bushy	Fernlike foliage; small pinkish white blooms
Tamarix pentandra	Tamarisk	T	Arching	Tightly packed small leaves in feathery fronds; tiny pink flowers

Deciduous shrubs
which prefer open situations

Caryopteris × clandonensis	Blue spiraea	S	Bushy	Grey-green, thin oval leaves; bright blue flowers
Helichrysum lanatum		S	Bushy	Silver-grey leaves; lemon yellow daisies
Hibiscus syriacus 'Duc de Brabant'	Tree hollyhock	M	Erect	Mid-green leaves; rose-purple trumpet flowers
Hibiscus syriacus 'Lady Stanley'	Tree hollyhock	M	Erect	Mid-green leaves; large white, pink-shaded flowers
Kolkwitzia amabilis	Beauty bush	M	Bushy	Small hairy leaves; small pink flower balls
Paeonia suffruticosa	Mountain peony	S	Loose, erect	Architectural leaves; large flesh-pink flowers
Perowskia atriplicifolia 'Blue Spire'	Russian sage	S	Bushy	Deeply cut grey-green leaves; lavender-blue flowers

CLIMBERS

This attractive relative of the potato – *Solanum crispum* 'Glasnevin' will climb successfully even in half shaded positions.

Evergreen climbers which tolerate heavy shade

LATIN NAME	COMMON NAME	DESCRIPTION
Hedera helix	Common ivy	Dark green classic ivy
Hedera helix 'Baltica'		Dark green classic ivy
Hedera helix 'Hibernica'	Irish ivy	Very large dark green ivy leaves

Evergreen climbers which tolerate half shade

Ceanothus arboreus 'Trewithen Blue'	Californian lilac	Mid-green oval leaves; deep blue flower panicles

LATIN NAME	COMMON NAME	DESCRIPTION
Clematis armandii		Shiny dark green foliage; waxy white flowers
Cytisus battandieri	Moroccan broom	Silvery green foliage; large yellow flower chains
Lonicera japonica 'Halliana'	Evergreen honeysuckle	Bright green oval leaves; white flowers
Trachelospermum jasminoides		Shiny dark green foliage; white jasmine-like flowers

Deciduous climbers
which tolerate heavy shade

Akebia quinata		Fragrant red racemes of flowers; five notched leaflets form composite leaf
Clematis alpina	Alpine virgin's bower	Deeply cut green foliage; open hanging blue bell flowers
Clematis montana		Four-petalled, single white or pink flowers; cut foliage
Clematis montana grandiflora		Green deeply cut foliage; white flowers
Clematis montana rubens		Dissected bronze foliage; strong pink flowers
Clematis tangutica		Lemon lantern flowers and wispy silver seed heads
Clematis 'John Warren'		Pale grey flowers with dark red edging
Lonicera japonica 'Aureo Reticulata'		Light green leaves with obvious gold veination
Lonicera × americana		Creamy honeysuckle flowers tinged with purple
Parthenocissus tricuspidata 'Veitchii'	Boston ivy	Three-lobed leaves; red in spring, dark green later
Rosa 'Zéphirine Drouhin'		Pink Bourbon-type flowers

Deciduous climbers
which tolerate half shade

Abutilon megapotamicum 'Kentish Bell'		Dark green slender leaves and orange bells
Aristolochia macrophylla	Dutchman's pipe	Large heart-shaped leaves; brownish yellow pitcher flowers

DECIDUOUS CLIMBERS WHICH TOLERATE HALF SHADE

LATIN NAME	COMMON NAME	DESCRIPTION
Clematis flammula		Bright bipinnate green leaves; small white flowers
Clematis orientalis		Silver-grey foliage and orange flowers
Hydrangea anomala petiolaris	Climbing hydrangea	Greenish white florets on broad corymbs
Jasminum officinale	Common white jasmine	Clusters of small white trumpets
Lonicera periclymtenum	Late Dutch honeysuckle	Rose purple honeysuckle flowers; yellow inside
Rosa 'Aimée Vibert'		Double white blooms; yellow stamens
Rosa 'Desprez à Fleur Jaune'		Apricot/yellow full blooms
Rosa 'Gloire de Dijon'		Buff yellow large globular blooms
Rosa 'La France'		Rose-pink deep cupped blooms
Rosa 'Madame Alfred Carrière'		White cupped blooms tinged with pink
Rosa 'Climbing Sombreuil'		Quartered blooms in creamy white
Solanum crispum 'Glasnevin'	Chilean potato tree	Bright purple 'nightshade' flowers; simple mid-green leaves
Vitis coignetiae		Very large dark green vine leaves

Sun-loving deciduous climbers

Actinidia kolomikta		Green heart-shaped leaves which become variegated cream and pink
Campsis radicans 'Flava'	Trumpet vine	Large green pinnate leaves; yellow trumpet flowers
Campsis radicans 'Madame Gallen'	Trumpet vine	Large green pinnate leaves; salmon pink trumpet-flowers
Clematis viticella		Dissected foliage; bell-shaped purple flowers
Passiflora caerulea	Passion flower	Palmate leaves; white and purple passion flowers
Wisteria sinensis	Wisteria	Large light green pinnate leaves; chains of mauve flowers

BULBS AND CORMS

S = less than 12 in (30 cm) high   M = 1–2 ft (30–60 cm)   T = 2 ft (60 cm) plus

Bulbs and corms tolerating half shade, or full shade if early flowering below a deciduous canopy

LATIN NAME	COMMON NAME	SIZE	FORM	DESCRIPTION
Allium ursinum		M	Erect	White flower 'globes'; curving straplike foliage
Anenome narcissiflora		M	Erect	Tufted foliage; white flowers with black stamens
Anemone nemerosa		S	Spreading	White anemone flowers
Anenome japonica 'Kriemhilde'	Windflower	T	Erect	Clear pink open flowers
Anemonopsis macrophylla		L	Bushy	Fernlike foliage; small white flowers with blue markings
Crocus chrysanthus 'Snow Bunting'		S	Rosettes	White faint indigo veining, orange spots
Cyclamen coum		S	Rosettes	Deep crimson and magenta flowers
Cyclamen neapolitanum		S	Rosettes	Small red cyclamen 'sails'
Cyclamen pseudibericum		S	Rosettes	Small rich red flowers
Cyclamen repandum		S	Rosettes	Carmine to soft rose pink flowers
Cyclamen neapolitanum 'Album'		S	Rosettes	Small white cyclamen 'sails'
Cyclamen persicum 'Dwarf Fragrance'		S	Rosettes	Small pink, red and white shades with red 'eyes'
Cyclamen 'Pastel Mixed'		S	Rosettes	Cream, white or pink cyclamen 'sails'
Erythronium dens-canis	Dog's tooth violet	S	Erect	Lilac, dark or light pink tiny violets
Fritillaria meleagris	Snakeshead	M	Erect	Nodding white chequered purple flowers
Galanthus nivalis	Snowdrop	S	Erect	Single white drooping flowers
Iris chrysographes		M	Erect	Violet-purple and yellow

BULBS AND CORMS TOLERATING HALF SHADE,
OR FULL SHADE IF EARLY FLOWERING BELOW A DECIDUOUS CANOPY

LATIN NAME	COMMON NAME			DESCRIPTION
Iris danfordiae		S	Erect	Lemon yellow flowers
Iris reticulata		S	Erect	Gold splashed mauve flowers
Lilium candidum	Madonna lily	T	Erect	Large white flowers
Lilium regale		T	Erect	White and yellow purple flushed flowers
Lilium speciosum rubrum		T	Erect	White flowers spotted crimson with very prominent stamens
Lilium auratum 'Lavender Princess'	Lily	T	Erect	Large lavender flecked creamy flowers
Lilium longiflorum 'White Queen'	Easter lily	T	Erect	Very large flared white flowers
Narcissus canaliculatus		S	Erect	Multiple heads of mini-daffodils with white petals and yellow cups
Narcissus jonquilla		M	Erect	Deep yellow jonquils
Narcissus 'April Tears'		S	Erect	Straplike leaves; yellow mini-daffodils
Narcissus 'Dove Wings'		M	Erect	Upright narrow green leaves and white narcissus flowers
Narcissus 'Geranium'		M	Erect	Pure white petalled narcissus with scarlet cups
Narcissus poeticus recurvus	Pheasant eye	M	Erect	Snow white petals sweep back from a yellow cup with red fringe
Narcissus 'Trevithian'		M	Erect	Multi-flowered lemon yellow narcissus
Scilla sibirica		S	Erect	Fleshy grass-like foliage; single blue bell-like flowers
Tulipa sylvestris	Woodland tulip	M	Erect	Clear yellow cups
Tulipa praestans 'Fusilier'	Meadow tulip	S	Erect	Multiple heads of orange cups

Bulbs and corms which enjoy open situations

Acidanthera bicolor 'Murielae'		T	Erect clump	Strong grass-like leaves; crimson blotched white flowers
Allium cernuum		M	Clump	Strap-like leaves; blue to pink globular umbels

Naturalised spring bulbs are one of the greatest delights in a woodland garden.

LATIN NAME	COMMON NAME			DESCRIPTION
Allium murrayanum		M	Clump	Strap-like leaves; rich pink multistemmed umbels
Allium pulchellum		M	Clump	Strap-like leaves; pink, red or purple umbels
Gladiolus carneus		M	Erect clump	White flowers with purple blotched lower petals
Iris pallida variegata		T	Erect fans	Grey-green leaves; yellow variegation; blue flowers
Iris kaempferi		T	Erect fans	White, blue or purple flowers
Iris foetidissima	Roast beef iris	M	Erect fans	Lilac flowers; prominent scarlet seed-pods

WATER PLANTS

S = less than 12 in (30 cm) high   M = 1–2 ft (30–60 cm)   T = 2 ft (60 cm) plus

Deciduous aquatic or bog plants which tolerate heavy shade

LATIN NAME	COMMON NAME	SIZE	FORM	DESCRIPTION
Gunnera manicata		T	Upright clumps	Gigantic dark green leaves; rusty brown spikes
Osmunda regalis	Flowering fern	T	Arching	Pale green fronds becoming russet in autumn

Deciduous aquatic or bog plants which tolerate half shade

Caltha palustris	Marsh marigold king cup	M	Branched tufts	Golden yellow cups
Lysichiton americanus	Skunk cabbage	M	Erect clumps	Large shiny leaves; yellow arum flowers
Nymphaea odorata 'Alba'	Water-lily	S	Floating	Lily pad foliage; pure white cup flowers
Nymphaea × marliacea 'Chromatella'	Water-lily	S	Floating	Lily pad foliage; glistening yellow cups
Nymphaea 'Firecrest'	Water-lily	S	Floating	Lily pad foliage; deep pink flowers
Pontederia cordata	Pickerel weed	M	Erect clumps	Large heart-shaped bright green leaves; small blue flowers
Rheum palmatum 'Rubrum'	Giant rhubarb	T	Erect clumps	Very large rhubarb-like reddish-brown leaves; creamy-white pink-tinged flowers

HERBACEOUS PLANTS

S = less than 12 ins (30 cm) high   M = 1–2 ft (30–60 cm)   T = 2 ft (60 cm) plus

Evergreen plants which tolerate heavy shade

LATIN NAME	COMMON NAME	SIZE	FORM	DESCRIPTION
Asplenium scolopendrium 'Undulatum'	Hart's tongue fern	T	Arching	Shiny crimped edged leaves
Fatsia japonica	Fig-leaf palm	T	Erect shrubby	Large dark green palmate leaves; milky white panicles
Lamium maculatum 'Chequers'		S	Spreading prostrate	Green leaves heavily spotted grey/green; white and purplish pink flowers
Pachysandra terminalis		S	Erect Shrubby	Shiny mid-green toothed foliage; nondescript whitish flowers
Vinca major	Greater periwinkle	M	Spreading	Dark green oval leaves; blue flowers
Vinca minor 'Bowles Variety'	Lesser periwinkle	S	Spreading	Small dark green leaves; bright blue flowers

Evergreen and semi-evergreen perennials which tolerate half shade

LATIN NAME	COMMON NAME	SIZE	FORM	DESCRIPTION
Avena candida (*Helictotrichon sempervirens*)		M	Hummocks	Blue-grey leaves; flowers make hazy plumes
Briza maxima (*Senecio maritimus*)	Quaking grass	M	Clumps	Grass leaves and graceful nodding flower stems
Cineraria maritima		S	Neat clump	Fern-like silver leaves
Dryas octopetala		S	Spreading	Small green oval leaves; cream white flowers with yellow centres
Dianthus plumaris 'Old Laced Pinks'	Cottage pinks	S	Clumps	Grey-green foliage; frilly pink flowers
Dianthus 'Mrs Sinkins'	Cottage pinks	M	Mounds	Silver foliage; maroon-eyed pink flowers
Eriophorum latifolium	Cotton grass	M	Clumps	Tufts of white 'cotton' on wiry stems
Festuca ovina glauca	Sheep's fescue	S	Tufts	Silvery blue grass
Iberis 'Snowflake'	Candytuft	M	Mounds	Small dark green leaves; white flowers

Few plants are more characteristic of a mature woodland garden floor than ferns and bluebells.

EVERGREEN AND SEMI-EVERGREEN PERENNIALS
WHICH TOLERATE HALF SHADE

LATIN NAME	COMMON NAME	SIZE	FORM	DESCRIPTION
Saxifraga cotyledon		S	Pendulous	Small green leaves; pinkish white flowers
Saxifraga 'Cloth of Gold'		S	Hummocks	Small golden leaves; white flowers
Sedum cauticolum		M	Tufts	Silver mounds; crimson floret sprays
Stachys lanata	Donkey's ears	M	Spreading	Silver felted leaves; pink flower spikes
Thymus serpyllum 'Coccineus'		S	Creeping mat	Thread-like fine foliage; red flowers

Evergreen perennials which enjoy full sun

Armeria caespitosa	Thrift	S	Hummocks	Narrow small green leaves; delicate pink globular flowers
Lavandula angustifolia	Lavender	T	Bushy	Silver grey foliage; silver blue flower spikes
Lithodora diffusa 'Heavenly Blue' Blue'		S	Trailing	Dark green needle-like leaves; deep blue flowers
Nepeta mussinii	Catmint	M	Clump	Small furry grey leaves; lavender blue flowers

Deciduous perennials
which tolerate heavy shade

Adiantum pedatum	Maidenhead fern	M	Clump	Radiating filigree of bright green leaflets
Artemisia 'Silver Queen'	Wormwood	T	Clump	Silver divided foliage; small yellow flowers
Brunnera macrophylla		M	Mound	Broad oval leaves; vivid blue sprays
Cimicifuga racemosa		T	Mat forming	Small green leaves; feathery tapering white tall flower spikes
Epimedium macranthum	Barren wort	S	Creeping	Attractive glossy leaves, bronzing in autumn
Hosta fortunei aurea		T	Clumps	Golden variegated leaves; mauve flower spikes
Hosta sieboldiana elegans		T	Clumps	Large crinkled blue green leaves; pale lilac flowers
Polygonatum multi-florum	Solomon's seal	T	Arching	Long fronds of light green leaves; drooping white bells

DECIDUOUS PERENNIALS WHICH TOLERATE HEAVY SHADE

LATIN NAME	COMMON NAME	SIZE	FORM	DESCRIPTION
Primula auricula 'Lovebird'	Auricula	S	Rosettes	Large waxy light green leaves; bright green petals with cream centre
Primula vulgaris	Primrose	S	Rosettes	Light green leaves; buttercup yellow flowers
Tiarella cordifolia	Foam flower	S	Clump	Golden leaves; foamy white flowers
Viola odorata 'Queen Charlotte'	Sweet violet	S	Clump	Small green oval leaves; small deep blue flowers
Viola 'Prince Henry'	Viola	S	Loose mound	Small green oval leaves; violet/purple flowers with gold throats

Deciduous perennials which tolerate half shade

Acanthus mollis		T	Clump	Glossy green; purple/white flowers
Acanthus spinosus	Bear's breeches	T	Arching clump	Dark green leaves; mauve flowers
Aconitum carmichaelii	Monkshood	T	Erect clump	Whorls of dissected green leaves; bright blue flowers
Aconitum fischeri	Aconite	T	Bushy	Whorls of dissected green leaves; purple flowers
Agrostis nebulosa	Cloud grass	M	Clumps	Wispy green foliage
Anaphalis margaritacea		M	Erect tufts	Silver foliage; loose white flower heads
Aquilegia caerulea	Rocky mountain columbine	M	Clump	Glaucous leaves; blue flowers
Aquilegia flabellata 'Pumila Alba'	Columbine	S	Clump	Glaucous leaves; white nodding flowers
Aruncus sylvester	Goat's beard	T	Clump	Small green leaves; creamy white flower heads
Astilbe 'Ostrich Plume'		T	Clump	Dissected green foliage; bright pink plumes
Astrantia major alba	Masterwort	M	Clump	Dissected green foliage; silver flowers with ruff-like bracts
Astrantia major alba 'Rozensymphonie'	Masterwort	M	Clump	Dissected green foliage; rose-tinged flowers
Campanula carpatica 'Blue'	Blue bellflower	M	Mound	Small mid-green leaves; blue upturned open bells
Campanula carpatica 'White'	White bellflower	M	Mound	Small mid-green leaves; white upturned open bells

LATIN NAME	COMMON NAME	SIZE	FORM	DESCRIPTION
Cardiocrinum giganteum		T	Erect	Several very large white trumpets on tall stems
Centranthus ruber	Red valerian	T	Erect, branching	Fleshy light green leaves; clusters of red or pink florets
Centranthus ruber 'Albus'	White valerian	T	Erect branching	Fleshy light green leaves; clusters of white florets
Convallaria majalis	Lily of the valley	S	Erect clumps	Long oval mid-green leaves; racemes of tiny white bells
Cortaderia selloana	Pampas grass	T	Erect clumps	Grass-like leaves; creamy white flower plumes
Dicentra formosa	Bleeding heart	M	Sprays	Fern-like foliage; mauve, pink or cream flower sprays
Dicentra spectabilis	Bleeding heart	T	Arching clumps	Finely divided foliage; white-tipped red flowers
Eryngium alpinum	Sea holly	M	Erect, branching	Blue-green marbled foliage; gun-metal blue flowers
Euphorbia wulfenii		T	Erect, shrubby	Grey-green foliage; bright yellow-green flowers
Helleborus niger	Christmas rose	M	Erect, branching	Glossy dark green leaves; gold-centred cream flowers
Hemerocallis 'Lark Song'	Day lily	T	Erect clump	Strap-like leaves; yellow trumpets
Lychnis coronaria 'Alba'	Campion	T	Mound	Silver-grey foliage; white flowers
Lychnis viscaria splendens plena	Campion	M	Loose clump	Thin grey-green leaves; magenta flowers
Malva alcea fastigiata	Mallow	T	Erect, bushy	Soft green foliage; soft pink flowers
Malva moschata alba	Mallow	T	Erect, bushy	Finely cut green leaves; large white flowers
Paeonia 'Kelways Lovely'	Peony	T	Erect clump	Green divided foliage; rose pink double flowers
Primula chionantha		M	Clump	Rosettes of light green leaves; white flower bunches
Primula denticulata alba		S	Erect	Rosettes of light green leaves; white flower globes
Primula veris	Cowslip	S	Erect	Rosettes of light green leaves; lemon yellow drooping flowers
Pulsatilla vulgaris	Pasque flower	S	Erect mounds	Feather foliage; open violet flowers

DECIDUOUS PERENNIALS WHICH TOLERATE HALF SHADE				
LATIN NAME	COMMON NAME	SIZE	FORM	DESCRIPTION
Pulsatilla vulgaris 'White'	Pasque flower	S	Erect mounds	Feathery foliage; open white flowers
Thalictrum dipterocarpum	Meadow rue	T	Branching erect	Small green leaves; pink petalled flowers; yellow stamens
Tiarella wherryi		S	Clump	Dissected gold foliage; pink flowers
Zantedeschia aethiopica 'Crowborough'	Arum lily	T	Erect clump	Large fleshy green leaves; white waxy trumpets

Sun-loving deciduous perennials

Achillea ageratifolia	Yarrow	M	Shrubby clump	Filigree green leaves; compact domes, white florets
Agapanthus patens	African lily	T	Clump	Strap-like leaves; clear blue flowers
Anemone pulsatilla (*Pulsatilla vulgaris*)	Pasque flower	M	Erect	Lacy grey foliage; mauve/red/purple cup flowers
Arabis alpina rosea	Pink arabis	S	Mound	Small narrow leaves; pink flowers
Arabis caucasica	Rock cress	M	Mound	Silver-grey leaves; white flowers
Campanula barbata alba	Alpine campanula	S	Mound	Small green leaves; small white bells
Campanula medium 'Bells of Holland'	Canterbury bell	M	Erect clump	Small green leaves; large blue/mauve/white bells
Catananche caerulea	Cupid's dart	M	Mound	Strap-like leaves; blue flowers
Centaurea montana	Knapweed	M	Clump	Silver-grey leaves; pink/violet/purple flowers
Chieranthus 'Bowles Mauve'	Perennial wallflower	M	Shrubby mound	Thin grey-green leaves; mauve flowers
Clematis integrifolia	Border clematis	T	Bushy mound	Small green leaves; blue bell flowers
Cosmos 'Sensation'		T	Loose clump	Ferny foliage; white/mauve/pink single yellow centred flowers
Crinum moorei	Cape lily	T	Erect	Green foliage; erect stems carrying white lily-like flowers
Crocosmia masonorum		T	Erect arching	Sword-like leaves; arching stems of orange flowers
Cynara cardunculus	Cardoon	T	Branched erect	Silver thistle-like foliage; large blue thistles
Delphinium hybridum 'Dwarf Snow White'		T	Erect	Small finely indented leaves; tall white flower spikes

Primroses and anemones are deciduous perennials which will tolerate sun or half shade and are typical of woodland edges.

LATIN NAME	COMMON NAME	SIZE	FORM	DESCRIPTION
Delphinium 'Blue Bees'	Larkspur	T	Erect	Finely indented leaves; tall blue flower spikes
Echinops ritro	Globe thistle	T	Erect clumps	Spiny blue grey leaves; steely blue globular flowers
Foeniculum vulgare	Fennel	T	Erect clumps	Feathery light green foliage; small yellow flowers
Geranium pratense		M	Spreading mound	Deeply dissected green leaves; pale blue open cups
Geranium wallickianum 'Buxton's Blue'	Hardy geranium	M	Spreading mound	Grey-green foliage; violet open cups
Geranium × 'Russell Prichard'	Crane's-bill	M	Spreading mound	Grey-green foliage, pink open cups
Gypsophila paniculata	Baby's breath	T	Bushy tangle	Small fine leaves; haze of small white flowers
Gypsophila 'Pink Star'	Baby's breath	M	Twiggy, tangled mound	Small green leaves; fog of pink star-like flowers

SUN-LOVING DECIDUOUS PERENNIALS

LATIN NAME	COMMON NAME	SIZE	FORM	DESCRIPTION
Linum perenne 'Blue Saphyr'	Blue flax	S	Mound	Grey-green leaves; sky blue single flowers
Linum perenne 'White Diamond'	White flax	S	Mound	Grey-green leaves; white single flowers
Matthiola bicornis	Night-scented stock	S	Erect	Thin mid-green leaves; single lilac flowers
Oenothera missouriensis	Evening primrose	M	Erect clump	Small oval leaves; bright yellow flowers
Papaver alpinum album	Alpine poppy	S	Erect clump	Light green furry foliage; white poppy blooms
Papaver orientae 'Goliath'	Oriental poppy	T	Loose clump	Jumble of fern-like foliage; large bright red poppies
Phlox douglasii	Alpine phlox	S	Mats	Dark green tiny leaves; pink/white flowers
Phlox paniculata 'Admiral'	Border phlox	T	Loose clump	Dark green leaves; spikes of white florets
Phlox paniculata 'Sandringham'	Border phlox	T	Loose clump	Dark green leaves; pink floret spikes
Physalis franchetii	Chinese lantern	M	Bushy	Green oval leaves; Orange 'lantern' seed-pods
Ranunculus gramineus	Buttercup	M	Clump	Grass-like foliage and yellow cups
Salvia argentea		M	Mound	Silver leaf rosettes; white/mauve flowers
Saponaria vaccaria 'Pink Beauty'		T	Arching sprays	Small green oval leaves; single pink flowers
Scabiosa caucasica	Scabious	T	Loose clump	Grey-green foliage; large lavender blue flowers
Scabiosa graminifolia		S	Mound	Silver grassy foliage; yellow-centred mauve flowers
Solidago 'Golden Thumb'	Dwarf golden rod	M	Bushy	Bright green bushy foliage; feathery yellow flower heads
Tradescantia 'Osprey'	Trinity flower	M	Clump	Rush-like shiny green leaves; three-petalled white flowers
Verbascum olympicum		T	Erect	Grey felty rosettes of foliage; gold flower spikes
Verbascum 'Gainsborough'		T	Erect clump	Silver leaves with pale yellow flower spikes
Veronica spicata incarna		M	Spreading	Grey foliage with violet flowers
Veronica virginica alba		T	Erect	Mid-green leaves; frail tall stems which terminate in white flower spires

Annuals and biennials which tolerate heavy shade

LATIN NAME	COMMON NAME	SIZE	FORM	DESCRIPTION
Impatiens 'Futura White'	Outdoor busy Lizzie	S	Mound	Small oval green leaves; single white flowers
Impatiens 'Futura Wild Rose'	Outdoor busy Lizzie	S	Mound	Small oval green leaves; single cherry red flowers
Lunaria annua alba	Honesty	M	Erect	Pointed oval leaves; white flowers; prominent seed-pods

Annuals and biennials which tolerate half shade

LATIN NAME	COMMON NAME	SIZE	FORM	DESCRIPTION
Antirrhinum 'Lavender Monarch'	Snapdragon	M	Erect	Dark green foliage; mauve snapdragon flowers
Antirrhinum 'Purple King'	Snapdragon	M	Erect	Dark green foliage; lilac purple flowers
Convolvulus major		T	Rambling	Triangular green leaves; white/pink/mauve/blue trumpets
Digitalis lanata	Foxglove	T	Erect clump	Silver leaves; pearl grey, yellow and purple-tinged bells
Digitalis purpurea alba	Foxglove	T	Erect clump	Large grey-green woolly leaves; spikes of white bells
Digitalis purpurea	Foxglove	T	Erect clump	Large grey-green woolly leaves; spikes of pink bells
Lathyrus odoratus 'Aerospace'	Sweet pea	T	Climbing	Light green oval leaves; large white flowers
Lathyrus odoratus 'Marietta'	Sweet pea	T	Climbing	Light green oval leaves; pinky mauve flowers
Lathyros odoratus 'Wiltshire Ripple'	Sweet pea	T	Climbing	Light green oval leaves; white flowers striped claret
Lunaria annua 'Munstead Purple'	Honesty	T	Erect	Velvety purple flowers; prominent silvery pods
Lupinus argenteus	Silver lupin	M	Erect	Silver-grey leaves; lilac flower spires
Lupinus 'Old Russell Blue'	Old garden lupin	T	Erect	Palmate leaves; blue flower spires
Myosotis sylvatica	Wood forget-me-not	M	Mound	Small green leaves; rich blue flowers
Nemophila menziesii	Baby blue eyes	S	Trailing	Finely dissected foliage; sky blue flowers

White flowered tobacco plants shine out against dark foliage and will thrive in either bright sun or half shade.

ANNUALS AND BIENNIALS WHICH TOLERATE HALF SHADE

LATIN NAME	COMMON NAME	SIZE	FORM	DESCRIPTION
Nicotiana affinis	Tobacco plant	T	Loose clump	Light green foliage; large white trumpets
Nicotiana alata 'Domino Scarlet'	Tobacco plant	T	Erect	Light green foliage; scarlet multiple trumpets
Nicotiana alata 'Dwarf White Bedder'	Tobacco plant	M	Low bushy	Small light green leaves; white multiple mini trumpets
Nicotiana alata 'Lime Green'	Tobacco plant	T	Bushy, erect	Light green leaves; lime green mini trumpets
Oenothera albicaulis 'Mississippi Primrose'	Evening primrose	M	Erect	Mid-green oval leaves; cream flowers fading to pink
Tropaeolum majus flora plena 'Orange Gleam'	Nasturtium	M	Open mound	Round green leaves; dark orange flowers
Tropaeolum nanum 'Empress of India'	Nasturtium	S	Open mound	Dark green round leaves; crimson flowers
Viola 'Baby Lucia'	Pansy	S	Loose clump	Small green leaves; small lavender flowers

Annuals and biennials which enjoy open situations

Argemone grandiflora	Prickly poppy	M	Clump	White veined prickly green leaves; large delicate white flowers
Ipomoea 'Heavenly Blue'	Morning glory	T	Climbing and rambling	Green ivy shaped leaves; clear blue trumpets
Lavatera trimestris 'Loveliness'	Rose mallow	T	Erect bush	Mid-green leaves; large pink flowers
Lavatera trimestris 'Silver Cup'	Mallow	T	Erect bush	Light green leaves; prominently veined silver-pink open cups
Nemesia 'Blue Gem'		S	Mound	Small green leaves; blue flowers
Nigella damascena 'Miss Jekyll'	Love-in-the mist	M	Clumps	Finely cut green foliage; clear blue flowers
Oenothera biennis	Evening primrose	S	Erect	Silver foliage; multiple yellow flowers
Papaver rhoeas	Poppy	M	Erect	Mid-green divided foliage; red cups, gold stamens
Papaver rhoeas 'Fairy Wings'	Poppy	S	Erect	Mid-green divided foliage; pastel shaded cups

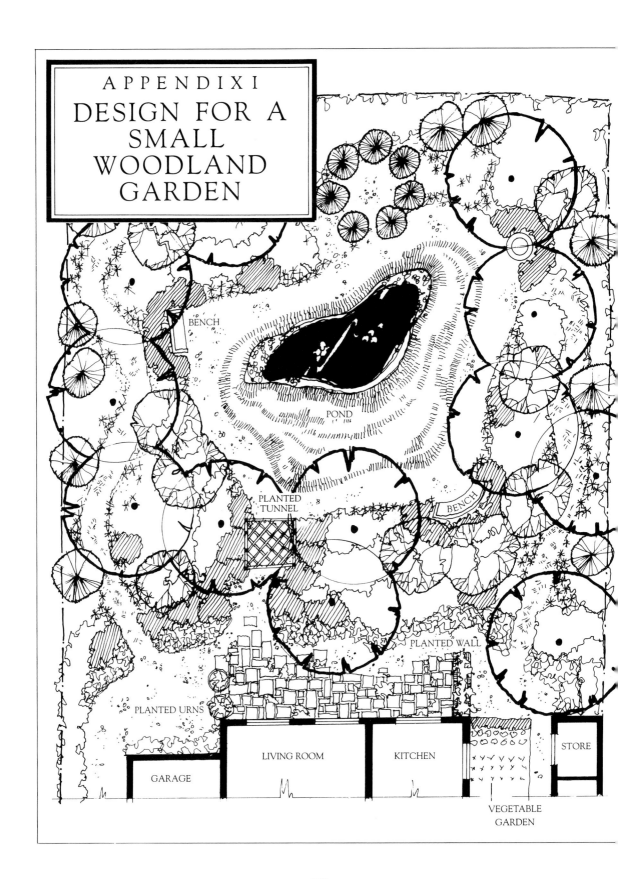

APPENDIX I
DESIGN FOR A SMALL WOODLAND GARDEN

BENCH

POND

PLANTED TUNNEL

BENCH

PLANTED WALL

PLANTED URNS

GARAGE

LIVING ROOM

KITCHEN

STORE

VEGETABLE GARDEN

Woodland gardening need not be confined to large multi-acred spreads. Even a plot as small as 1/20th acre (50 ft deep × 45 ft wide) which is commonplace in many suburbs could become a sylvan place if laid out and planted as shown in this notional design (see left).

On such a restricted site there would only be room for one true glade and that would also have to contain a pond feature. However something resembling a second glade with its more open character could be created by making the terrace next to the house very generous, paving it rather formally and allowing it to blend gradually with the paths leading from it by sinking a few further paving stones into their coarse grit surface.

In this design, apart from the more formal central pathway round the garden from the light terrace area through a dark curtain of trees out into the light glade, there is a second, softer bark-topped woodland perimeter track on which much of the time visitors would be under the dark canopy of trees.

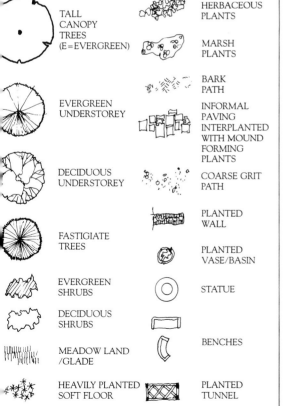

TALL CANOPY TREES (E=EVERGREEN)	HERBACEOUS PLANTS
	MARSH PLANTS
	BARK PATH
EVERGREEN UNDERSTOREY	INFORMAL PAVING INTERPLANTED WITH MOUND FORMING PLANTS
DECIDUOUS UNDERSTOREY	COARSE GRIT PATH
	PLANTED WALL
FASTIGIATE TREES	PLANTED VASE/BASIN
EVERGREEN SHRUBS	STATUE
DECIDUOUS SHRUBS	
MEADOW LAND /GLADE	BENCHES
HEAVILY PLANTED SOFT FLOOR	PLANTED TUNNEL

**APPENDIX II
RULES OF THE
SUNDAY TIMES
WOODLAND
GARDEN DESIGN
COMPETITION**

Entrants to this competition are asked to suggest a design to transform the area of the Chelsea Hospital grounds shown on the attached scaled and contoured plan into a woodland garden.

The site already possesses several mature trees whose canopies and species are indicated on the plan. They lightly shadow what is at present mown grass. It is hoped that it will be possible to leave some of this grass unmown for a few weeks prior to the Chelsea Show should the winning design include meadow areas.

The judges will be looking for a design which strikes a good balance between the elements implicit in the competition title. While they hope that the design when built will convey a natural woodland feeling it should also ultimately become the type of garden which would provide an ongoing interest in its maintenance and development for keen gardeners.

The overall winner will receive a cash prize of £500 and have the pleasure of seeing his/her design brought to life at Chelsea. The second and third prizewinners will receive £300 and £200 respectively and will be the guests of *The Sunday Times* at the Chelsea Show. The first prizewinning design will be featured in the pre-show issue of *The Sunday Times* Magazine.

The competition will be judged by television gardener Peter Seabrook, Doctor Laurie Boorman of the Institute of Terrestrial Ecology, Harry Hartley – Marketing Director, Marshalls Mono Ltd., Arthur George, Managing Director, Hydon Nurseries Ltd., Rosemary Alexander, Principal, The English Gardening School, and Michael Miller, Managing Director of Clifton Nurseries Ltd.

COMPULSORY FEATURES

Designs submitted for the Competition should include the following compulsory features:-

1. Suggestions for an entrance gate to the garden. Visitors to the stand will follow a one way system.

2. Suggestions for an exit gate.

3. Suggestions for a fence along the north east border of the garden (between the Hydon site and the picnic area) which would enable people moving along the path outside to see into the garden.

4. The track of a path through the garden (to be made of 'unwashed' gravel) with a minimum width of 4 ft leading from the entrance to the exit of the garden. To ensure access for wheelchair gardeners no slope on the path should be too steep.

5. The location and design of a simple opensided 'loggia' type tranquil sitting area to be built in Marshalls' 'Heritage' Old York walling with a timber and wood shingle roof. This building should be large enough to accommodate a 5 ft bench, 2 armchairs and a 30 in diameter table from Marshalls' 'Rosedale' collection of hardwood furniture. It should be located on a suitably scaled surrounding terrace made from Marshalls' 'Heritage' Old York paving slabs and could be defined by low planted walls and include provision for other appropriate planting.

6. A small scale appropriate pond feature.

7. The location of 12 largish trees drawn from the following:-

Acer	– *platanoides*
	– *p.* 'Crimson King'
	– *campestre*
Aesculus	– *carnea* 'Briotti'
Sorbus	– *aria* 'Lutescens'
	– *intermedia*
Tilia	– *cordata*
	– *euchlora*
	– *platyphyllus*

8. The location of 6 largish trees drawn from flowering Prunus and Malus varieties.

Statuary in woodland gardens always looks well when it is particularly screened by foliage so that visitors are obliged to approach it to be able to appreciate it completely.

9. The location of 30 large specimen shrubs drawn from:-
Acer-palmatum types and *palmatum* 'Dissectum'

Rhododendrons in variety
Azaleas in variety
Viburnums in variety
Skimmia in variety
Camellia in variety
Elaegnus in variety
Mahonia in variety
Osmanthus in variety
Enkianthus campanulatus
Pieris formosa forrestii

10. The location of patches of the wildflowers shown on the following list:-

Rosa canina
Endymion non-scripta
Geranium pratense
Betonica officinalis
Hypericum hirsutum
Primula vulgaris
Caltha palustris
Lychnis flos-cuculi
Primula veris
Narcissus spp

OTHER FEATURES
Within the bounds of appropriateness, apart from the compulsory plants entrants are free to include other small ornamental trees and shrubs to enrich the planting and to include other herbaceous plants such as ferns, astilbes, hostas, ivies, foxgloves and primula hybrids.

Apart from the compulsory hard-topped path, entrants are free to indicate where they would mow other pathways through the long grass.

PLANTING AT CHELSEA
While naturally the judges will be looking for a design which will look good during the period of the Chelsea Flower Show, entrants are reminded that the planting in their design should be capable of offering interest over a long season.

While every effort will be made to ensure that the planting in the garden made at Chelsea conforms as far as possible to that suggested by the winning entrant it is not always possible to obtain particular plants. Entrants are therefore asked to

accept that changes may have to be made at the organisers' discretion.

Whenever possible these will be made after consultation with the winner.

THE SUBMISSION
Entrants should submit clear plans and whenever possible perspective drawings mounted on thin boards measuring no more than 24 in x 18 in.

To supplement the drawings, entrants may include typewritten descriptions of their designs, to a maximum length of 500 words.

Each sheet in the submission must be clearly labelled with the entrant's name, address and telephone number. No entrant may submit more than one design.

Groups are permitted to work on single entries but prizes will be awarded only to the individual representing the group whose name appears on the submission.

Entrants should note that their entries will not be returned.

CO-SPONSORS
Apart from its 'Heritage' Old York walling which proved so popular a feature of *The Sunday Times* stand at the 1986 Chelsea Flower Show, for this competition Marshalls Mono Ltd. of Halifax will be supplying items from its 'Rosedale' range of excellent hardwood furniture. The garden at Chelsea will be built by Clifton Nurseries Ltd., the London landscapers which carried off a Gold Medal at the 1986 show.

By collaborating in landscaping the margins of its traditional stand to make them appear as a dense and beautiful shrubbery on one border of the prize-winning garden and supplying some of its superbly grown rhododendrons and azaleas for enriching the general planting, Hydon Nurseries Ltd. will do much to improve the woodland garden made at Chelsea.

In conjunction with wildflower seed specialist John Chambers of Kettering the Institute of Terrestrial Ecology has agreed to rear appropriate wildflowers for the woodland garden.

The organisers of the competition are grateful to Rosemary Alexander, Principal of The English Gardening School at the Chelsea Physic Garden for making a detailed survey of the competition site and preparing the plan.

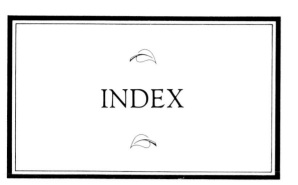

INDEX